METAFISH

DARREL ROBERT SPENST

Thanks for reading the book!

DISCLAIMER

This book is full of conjecture. (And perhaps full of something else as well, but even a litter box can be easily cleaned if the litter sifts nicely and the container is sufficiently sturdy.) The enclosed speculations may be helpful to you. Or they may not. Feel free to disregard them. Or even more free to regard them.

Caveat lector, reader beware: this is a work of fiction, speculation, and even -- occasionally -- fact. However, sizable portions of such fact are autobiographical. They therefore draw upon this author's imperfect memory, the same memory which occasionally forgets to feed the family cat precisely on schedule.

All Bible quotes reference the King James Version, unless otherwise noted.

No animals were harmed in the making of this construct. (However, the family cat verged on discomfort once or twice. *Selah*.)

Copyright (C) 2019 by Darrel Robert Spenst

ISBN 978-0-9865485-1-2 (pbk)

All rights reserved. Published by PAINTSMITHink.

www.PAINTSMITHink.com

Cover design by Colton Floris

(coltonfloris.com)

TABLE OF CONTENTS

Preface	7
Dedication	17
Epigrapha	19
Chapter 1: Fish	21
Chapter 2: Dog	41
Chapter 3: Cat	57
Chapter 4: Cow	67
Chapter 5: Bird	79
Chapter 6: Snake	89
Chapter 7: Donkey	107
Chapter 8: Bee	115
Chapter 9: Camel	127
Chapter 10: Rooster	137

Chapter 11: Sheep	153
Chapter 12: Goat	165
Chapter 13+14: Grasshopper/Ant	177
Chapter 15: Horse	191
Chapter 16: Rabbit	203
Chapter 17: Spider	217
Chapter 18: Pig	229
Chapter 19: Elephant	247
Chapter 20: Armadillo	261
Chapter 21: Wolf	271
Chapter 22: Fox (and Coyote)	285
Chapter 23: Tiger	297
Chapter 24: Lion	315
Epilogue	327

PREFACE

This is not a book of parables. It was meant to be. All the intentions were there. They were good intentions, great, perhaps even the best. But then, well, the cows got out of the barn, so to speak. And they began to speak. (So to speak.) And not only cattle.

Parables, by definition, do not feature talking animals. This restriction hindered my fictional animals not at all. It was rudely ignored. Indeed, it was trampled upon. Through no fault of my own — besides having written them — the narrative representations set forth in this book were overrun by these chatty creatures. Intended as order, chaos emerged, a zoo with broken bars and open cages. But then again, perhaps more than a zoo; perhaps a circus. For that creative reality strikes the better balance between anarchy and harmony, bridled and unbridled in equal measure in service to a generative interplay woven as a safety net under the spiritual trapeze artist's aerial acrobatics and the highwire of Being. However, it is what it is. I will not quarrel with it. After all, even God can speak through an ass. He might even use donkeys.

But how to describe this book, if not as a book of parables? Perhaps as a collection of fables? The talking animals criterion is certainly met, however the human component anomalizes the standard fabulatory delimitation. Does that mean what I think it means? It might. But that goes for a lot of things. The point is, there are human beings involved in these brief stories, doing their things, and playing their parts, as we all surely do during the brief time given to us upon this strangely generative earth. As do the animals. The resulting genre is what some might call a dog's breakfast. But a dog's breakfast is still breakfast, even if one is only a dog. (See Chapter 2.) And that is meant in the best way possible.

What then should these literary fusions be named, if not fables, if not parables? Perhaps fablables? Farables? Pables? Oh, my Lord — this is music to no one's ears. But wait — there is another option. Out of readerly kindness, grant me this: the word "parafabula" (*pair-uh-FAB-yew-luh*), a melding of two different linguistic elements: the Greek "para" (from which the word "parable" is partially derived), and the Latin "fabula" (from which the word fable is derived). The singular, of course, would be "parafabulon" (*pair-uh-FAB-yew-lawn*). Why not? An animalgam, a comanthropound, a protosynthesis.

However, not only is this book a compilation of parafabula. As with vision, there is more to the eye than meets the eye. There is an underlying structure. But I am talking about this book. Each chapter follows a similar framework of expanding visualization: first a *parafabulon* featuring a specific interpretive animal initiates a motion or movement; then a *ruminatio* (*roo-min-AY-show*) — an imaginative chewing over, a tumbling in the mind, a mental rock polishing via refining cerebral grit — both encircles and propagates beyond. As a pebble tossed into still water generates ever-expanding rings of interest, so the parafabulon begets patterns of meditation and rumination. Or, at least, that is the fundamental idea. I have little to say about such disorderly complications as rocks hurled across wind-scoured surfaces, or boulders tumbled into rushing waters, or monoliths levered off cliffs into vast tidal pools. Those without sin may cast such stones, for this book represents a more modest form of casting. This is pebble level. This is still water level. But sometimes (now, I propose) less may be more.

If this parafabulous (*pair-uh-FAB-yew-luss*) anthology assumes the likeness of (*uv*) an interpretive zoo (as mentioned previously), well, I have tried to close some cage doors and open others. In truth, some will not close and others will not open. To see it as a metaphorical menagerie of meaning, fraught with figural fauna for reflection, is certainly permissible, though I will never use this sentence again. But if it gives the impression of a traveling contemplative circus (as previously mentioned), this writer's delight will know no bounds, for in its rings of ludic bemusement there are beasts both wild and tame, mortals both perplexed and perplexing.

The natural world is a clear and compelling apologetic for the spiritual world, for in the same way that microscopic organisms like tardigrades — invisible "water bears" populating an unseen (to us) ecosphere — exist in nested ignorance within the plant domain, and plants exist in nested ignorance within the animal kingdom, and animals exist in nested ignorance within human society, so too do humans exist in nested ignorance within what some might call angelic hierarchies. There is no reason to assume we are not the tardigrades of some higher reality. In fact, it seems more likely than not we are existentially situated within some layer of limited perception circumscribed by the restrictive limits of our natural forms. Like our family cat observing us tapping away on electronic devices or driving around in baffling machinery, we are blind and uncomprehending to that which is clearly visible, for we do not commonly have the means of understanding it. No wonder a prophetic glimpse into the spiritual realm is called a vision. And no wonder we need the salt of Scripture's subsequent witness to gain traction on our path through the spiritual world, for it alone can lower the freezing point of that frictionless reality to the point where we can begin to get a grip on fundamental truth.

Can words strictly arranged in sequence accomplish such allusive traction or evoke the carnivalesque ambiguity this book desires? Perhaps. One can only hope, for words are slippery things. They get old. They get tired. They lose their freshness. And sometimes they lose their meaning. Or change their meaning. Words are a medium. (Is it any wonder their magic is produced by spelling?) Books are made of words in the same way paintings are made of paint. (Something with which this writer is very familiar, having spent many years manipulating brush and paint in the service of detailed decorative and artistic embellishment.) And in the same way certain pigments are susceptible to fading in sunlight, words are subject to bleaching and discoloration due to lengthy cultural exposure. Some words are more durable than others. However, all are vulnerable not only to the predations of time, but also to the irrepressible fertility of the human imagination. (Not to mention the acidity of corrosive ideologies and the lexical horror of vitriolic cultural malevolence.)

Actions might speak louder than words, but words speak farther. Without them, actions would not be broadcast beyond their immediate moment. Words are intricate tools we take for granted, for indeed they have been granted. We need words. And we need new words. New words can be to language what fresh leaves are to trees. How else to synthesize ongoing developments in the cultural and technological atmosphere? How else to renovate concepts whose words are so attenuated, so weak in effect, so deficient in any real explanatory power, so corrupted by seasonal interpretive interactions, that their original purpose no longer does duty?

This is where one such as myself should say something about Shakespeare, for it seems one must always mention Shakespeare in relation to the ingenious use and inexhaustible invention of words. Indeed, the man -- if indeed he was a man -- coined more than a thousand words in the English language alone. He also wrote the King James Bible. However, one of the preceding sentences is not true. But only if we are talking strictly about facts.

It has been said nothing persists which is not of spirit; that spirit precedes materiality. Or maybe what we experience as "material" is really just information given shape. Material reality is subject to entropy and degeneration. From Vincent van Gogh's "Flowers in a Blue Vase" with its varnish greying over the cadmium yellow blossoms, to Leonardo da Vinci's original masterpiece "The Last Supper" flaking off its wall due to the failure of experimental technique and excess humidity, the integrity of a masterwork may from time to time require the attention of an expert conservator.

Is traditional Christianity — for this is what I have been leading up to this whole time, talking about animals and whatnot — itself a masterwork in need of such conservation? It is certainly possible, for I have learned from my own kitchen cabinets that white does not stay white without effort. It may also be fair to argue that Christianity is a painting which has never been completed. Such could be the picture of faith. So then: is it simply a matter of removing the old obscuring varnish here and there? Or does one paint in or paint out whole sections? And who is qualified to perform such work? I am not so sure. I have certainly seen it attempted in the past by those with insufficient skill or wisdom. Even an experienced conservator may not be capable of removing the varnish without damaging the underlying composition. Or may not have skill or talent enough to paint in the fresh colors and forms. Perhaps a minimal cleaning and fresh coat of varnish is all one can hope for. Time will tell.

In the meantime, this amateur conservator's touch will fall

upon only two specific words: "Christian" and "Christianity" themselves. These words have become so general, so common, so overused — who knows what they even mean anymore? Not only to those who use them, but also to those who claim them. What was once uniquely — and simultaneously — inclusive and exclusive in its distinction has become only loosely descriptive in application. Throughout this book of parafabula I propose to substitute for them the somewhat less familiar words "Christer" (CRY-stir) and "Christerica" (krist-AIR-ika) as a way to read their original meaning afresh, to delineate something more foundational, something abstracted from the convoluted composition currently set before us. (Except when the old words are used in their old context.)

"Christer" refers not only to a state of Being, but also to one of Doing. A noun, yes. But also a verb. A Christer "Christs". Just like a painter paints. Following Christ is an activity — Christing. "To Christ" is to function in specific ways. These ways will become apparent in the course of this book. Or not. My claims are very modest. I am only speaking out loud. (So to think.) It is all simply a peculiar exposition of that definition. And to be clear, I am not trying to redefine what it means to be a "Christian" per se, for I have chosen only to suspend that word temporarily, as a coach substitutes one player for another. The word "Christian" is on the bench, and the word "Christer" is in the game. Let us observe how it plays. For I am simply defining what it means to be a "Christer". But I do hope that for many who are fans of

"Christian", it will not be too difficult a matter to imaginatively embrace this new player, and to contemplate a more refined and fundamental designation previous to dogmatic denominational overlay or ritualistic regulatory restriction.

The second word, "Christerica", simply describes the spiritual incorporation of all Christers, for all true Christers are part of a mystical Body transcending race, language, gender, culture, and time. And space. And probably a lot more. Christers form Christerica, the Body of Christ. There is no other Christerica than the one formed by Christers themselves. No building, denomination, music, creed, symbol, ritual, or liturgy is required to add or admit the Christer to Christerica, only faith in Christ itself, through God's grace. The rest is all aesthetics, surface decoration, dabs of highlighting, varieties of fellowship, styles of worship. These are not the structure itself. The Master-piece is essentially and fundamentally one's "unvarnished" (Shakespeare again) soul, in Christ, in spiritual fellowship with every other unvarnished soul in Christ, the hidden manifestation of a metaphysical cross-linking similar to that found in the chemical properties of various compatible painting mediums. Decorative or preservative application comes later, and may be changed — and often is — at a moment's cultural notice.

What am I even talking about? If a ceremonial varnish of protective ritual is desired, it is only applied to a completed work, as any painter well knows. What else? A removable varnish — subject to dissolution by the appropriate Spirit — is the technically correct coating to employ.

PREFACE

The following work is not a systematic theology, nor is it a coherent philosophical system. (Shoot — it might not even be readable.) But neither is it without plan or direction, for who rides a horse with their eyes closed? It is more a series of improvisational riffs upon a structure of harmonic themes using writing as the instrument and animals as the grounding melodies. As jazz theologian — and pianist — Nelson Boschman has said, "We need both limitation and liberation, and we need to hold them in proper tension."[1] For we know perfect law brings freedom.[2]

Some of this may seem awkward at first. And perhaps later as well, for not everyone likes syncopated harmony. But this is only speaking in metaphor. However, imagery — like an animal in an ark — loves company. So let us also say there is no view at the bottom of a ladder, and words are the rungs used to ascend. Sir Edmund Hillary did not climb Mount Everest by staying in base camp. And neither did his climbing partner, Tenzing Norgay. One foot must be placed in front of the other for the summit to be reached.

I myself sat in a chair. At my desk. In my study. Eating crackers for sustenance.

For my mountain was this book, the summit its completion, and the anticipated reader my imaginative climbing partner, without whose silent collaboration these words would only be stones of potential, littering a disorderly home study base camp of uncollated notes and unallocated scribbles.

Pause and consider.

DEDICATION

To my fellow Pisciculi*

(*Little Christer-fishes...)**

[**...*Follow me, and I will make you fishers of men.* (Jesus Christ, Matthew 4:19)]

EPIGRAPHA

But the hour cometh, and now is, when the true worshippers shall worship the Father in spirit and in truth…

(Jesus Christ, *John 4:23*)

…The word is nigh thee, even in thy mouth, and in thy heart: that is, the word of faith, which we preach; That if thou shalt confess with thy mouth the Lord Jesus, and shalt believe in thine heart that God hath raised him from the dead, thou shalt be saved.

(Apostle Paul, *Romans 10:8-9*)

…you could say…in some sense that Christ is a META-FISH. A fish is something that you can dine on, but a way of being is something that provides you with something to dine on on a continual basis.

(Jordan Peterson, *Maps of Meaning* lecture series, YouTube, 2017)

CHAPTER 1

FISH

<u>PARAFABULON</u>

Two fish swam in the sea. There were many dangers in the sea, and they were afraid.

A Fish they did not know appeared unto them.

"Do not be afraid," said the Fish.

"But we are afraid," said the two fish.

"Do not be afraid — I am the Metafish."

"Still afraid."

"I am the Metafish. Do not be afraid. I created you."

"Wait…"

"I laid the foundations of this world, and spoke its life into existence."

"You…"

"I have spoken."

"Why have you come to us, Metafish?"

"To tell you what you do not know."

"What do we not know?"

"That you exist in water."

"What is water?"

"It is what you cannot see, but that which you cannot live without."

"Where is it, this water of which you speak?"

"It is all around you."

"We cannot see it."

"Come, I will show you."

The Metafish carried them up out of the water and into the sky.

"There is the water below," said the Metafish.

"What is this place we are in now, then?" said the two fish.

"It is the air."

"What is the air?"

"It is not water. You cannot live here. Without me, you could not breath, and would die."

"How can this be?"

"I am the Metafish. With me, all things are possible."

The Metafish then carried them over the moon, around the sun, and throughout distant stars. The entire world would not be big enough to contain all the books needed to describe the things the Metafish showed them and said unto them.

"How can all this be?" said the two fish.

"It has been spoken," said the Metafish.

"And now where will you take us?"

"I will take you back to the water."

"And why?"

"That is where you live."

"But we would live with you," said the two fish.

"Who do you say that I am?"

"You are the Metafish."

"You will not die in water."

"When will we live with you?" said the two fish.

"Not yet, but now," said the Metafish.

"Not yet, but now," said the two fish, "not yet, but now. How do we live in the not yet, but now?"

"Exactly as if the not yet were now, for now is not yet and not yet is now."

"I mean…"

"Tell others what you have seen and learned."

"They will not believe us."

"Who do you say that I am?"

"You are the Metafish."

"Tell others. I will return for those who believe in the life of the Metafish, creator of water, air, and star."

"They will not believe us, and we will die."

"You will not die in water, and neither will they, if they would abide in me."

At this, the Metafish vanished. Or at least, was no longer visible.

The two fish went and told others of the Metafish and all the marvellous things they had seen.

The others did not believe, though some did.

And in time, the two fish died.

And the Metafish was seen no more.

RUMINATIO

I know a person very well who, when she was a child, was fascinated by the minnows swimming in the slough behind her home. She would go out early in the morning — when the dawn was just barely breaking upon the fog-furled and dew-bejewelled world of her youth, long before the rest of her family, even her father, had begun to stir from their night's sleep — in an effort to catch the minnows.

She did not wish to harm the minnows. She bore no ill will towards them. Rather, she was simply overwhelmed with a profound curiosity and a vague but compelling desire to establish some manner of connection, however tenuous, with the transcendent beauty glittering up from the depths.

For she loved the minnows deeply, in the way only a child can. They flashed like fine gems, intricately cut and colored, yet provocatively alive. They were like candy and gum, firecrackers and confetti. They seemed quicksilver signifiers — though such words would have been farther from her young grasp than the minnows themselves — embodying concrete but wordless solutions to the cloud of mystery which surrounded her young self with an enchantment she could not fully understand, though indeed it made its appearance on every side, and her young eyes saw nothing else, for there was nothing else to see but a constant succession of mind-igniting and soul-kindling manifestations parading past in one continuous vision.

Upon occasion, she would actually — small miracle! — catch a minnow, and holding it in her sturdy little hands, would observe it closely, solemnly running a careful forefinger along its iridescent side as it struggled in the foreign atmosphere.

Very quickly then, she would toss it back into the murky water and watch with serious delight as it sped away, flashing down into the concealing deep. And she would continue to simply squat — her eyes shining — at the water's edge, with her elbows upon her knees, and her chin upon her hands, marvelling at the obscure watery world before her.

I am told those who fish for sport — for I myself am not familiar with such activity — derive their interest from a similar sense of wonder, mystery, and enigmatic questing which the little girl above experienced, though conducted on a much larger and more involved scale. And having once lived in the southern portion of the state of Florida myself, I am well aware of those who have such ineluctable attractions to tarpon, sailfish, swordfish, and the like. Indeed, I too have seen many things in ocean waters — elephantine aggregations of grazing sea cows (commonly known as manatee), roiling clouds of stingrays, jellyfish by the gelatinous hundreds — to marvel at, for I have followed the wind on many a nautical excursion, a sailboard stiff-finned and directionally surgical beneath my feet, a light, powerful, uncomplicated sail — shaped perfectly by carbon fiber mast and boom — alive in my hands, baptizing me with the power to transcendently skim across the white-capped surface of the fathomless deep.

Before that, however — and long ago it now seems — I too was a child enchanted by the mystery in which I found myself enveloped, an unlikely wanderer in Andean mists (which was exactly the literal case, upon occasion), also irresistibly seeking things I could not name. But I had no watery backyard world to explore. Indeed, my boyhood sloughs were dry, sun-baked, palm-shaded, adobe-walled. My childhood minnows were motionless and adamantly present, though no less elusive for all that. My rainbows were gritty, my shadows replete with elusive interplays of light, my surfaces ruined by time and by an unstoppable entropy whose visual effects were as never-ending as the ongoing progression of their causal moments. My iridescent fish were spectrums of dirt, colors in the public market, and textures on every sidewalk, building, and road. Every tree had its bark and every flower its petal; every vehicle its rust and every bench its blemish. Tarnish and patina were ever-present reminders of what I could nevertheless not avoid, for my perceptions were unaccountably attuned to such detailed imperfection.

But slough girl and I, we were both seeking the Metafish in our own way, and — in our own way — each found our way. Small revelation we married one another, for faith and wonder are both powerfully attractive — and synergistic — forces of the very highest order. But enough romance for now.

The title of this book — and the parafabulon above — introduces a linguistic, metaphorical, and metaphysical organism of seemingly unlimited significance. For Christ — like the positive catalyst added to a solution to precipitate a chemical reaction — is the agent of change titrating this dramatic suspension in which we exist, hardening reality with a Christalline metastructure, the solution within a solution, the precipitating precipitate. Unscriptural platitudes undermining both the predatory and pastoral nature of this Being must be laid at the feet of the Man and Master we call Jesus Christ, along with every other prejudice and pretension. For the Metafish is a sharp creature, an astringent being, nothing fishy about it, scales for weighing, prey for praying. Not so much a minnow, as a winnow. Not — definitely not — religiously ornamental: rather, an ultimate reality, an incarnate instrument, a refiner's fire. Unschooled, it schools. Uncreated, it creates. Meta, yes, definitely; met a yes, definitively. And so on.

But after all, what is this "meta"? What is this interpretive thing I have fished out of the linguistic sea? It seems this Greek prefix "meta" is everywhere these days, unleashed like some invasive postmodern species into the ecosystem of contemporary language. We have metamovies, metabooks, metadata. That is, movies about movies, books about books, data about data, not to mention discourse about discourse, thoughts about thoughts, words about words, and so on.

Maybe it is not surprising that a culture of entitlement and narcissism finds a seemingly endless fascination with everything self-referential. The world is slowly turning in upon itself. God is far away or non-existent. And Jesus Christ? Well, he has been gone a long time. Maybe he is not coming back at all. Or maybe he never even existed. Best to forget about all that, say some. Get on with things. Human things. Earthly things.

Partially lost in the current meta-fad is a more foundational use of the "meta" prefix, the one meaning "beyond". As in "metaphysical", that which is beyond the physical. In other words, spiritual.

Followers of Christ have been on board with this "meta" for a long time. It is exactly the "meta" that takes us beyond ourselves into a more genuine reality. (In fact — forgive me — the Metafishical.) We all know that someday our miraculous and awe-inspiring bodies will ultimately fail and die. Some of us even feel it. Indeed, the life we live is similar to the life of a plant or crop. No wonder the collection of books we call the Bible uses wheat so often as imagery for humanity. Like wheat, this life is our one chance to grow and bear seed. Whether we do so or not, the plant of our bodies will eventually wither and die. How wonderful if that inescapable narrative arc not only develops character and yields a bountiful harvest in the fields of our mortal existence, but also accomplishes the inner transformation required to viably exist in the heavenly realm, a happy ending that is in truth the right and proper beginning.

Over the centuries, Christ has been represented by the fish symbol. It is everywhere. Just google "fish symbol" as an image search, or take a drive around town. Chances are one will not make it back home without seeing a Jesus fish — or its natural predator, the Darwin fish — on the rear bumper of some other vehicle. (Who ever thought Satan could be so clever?)

The Greek word "ichthys" ("fish") is a type of acrostic for the phrase "Jesus Christ, Son of God, Savior". The fish was also a symbol early Christians could use instead of the cross to escape the notice of their persecutors, since it was a symbol that pre-dated Christianity, and therefore might not arouse the suspicion of the authorities. There have always been fish — in the sea, yes, but also in the imagination. The Bible itself is a kettle of fish. Its interpretive net is filled with fish-related imagery, ranging from the whale in the story of Jonah[3] all the way through to some of the miracles of Christ. (The first miraculous haul,[4] the feeding of the five thousand,[5] the fish with the coins in its mouth,[6] the second miraculous haul.)[7] The Master went so far as to call his disciples "fishers of men".[8] (And there is no need to even mention here the zodiacal idea of the "Age of Pisces" which coincides with Christ and the life of his Church. Sort of. I am no astrologer, but I do know pisces means fish.)

The fruitful notion of Christ as Metafish, Christ as a way of being, sounds about right, meta enough for me, a fabulous Fish tale from head to...tail. And the allusion in the epigraph to the historic Christian rite of communion — "something to dine on" — is obvious. The role of ritual and sacrament in the Christer life is a topic overripe for discussion, and may even be fruitful. I will come back to it later.

The parafabulon at the head of this chapter expresses a truth we often overlook in the busyness of our everyday lives. (Besides the one that just because something is not currently visible, does not mean it is imaginary. For example...well, fish. And Christ. And love. And many other things too obvious to mention.)

That truth is this: the history of the world for the last two thousand years is — from a Christian perspective — the history of the non-return of Christ. For those who follow the Master, everything in heaven and earth is about Christ, one way or another, whether anyone denies it or accepts it, for denial of reality does not alter reality in the slightest, and subjectivity only relatively affects objectivity.

The passage of time allows for — indeed, encourages — the proliferation of imaginative constructs. Nature abhors a vacuum and apparently so do we. Time is a container which will be filled with one thing or another. And two thousand years is a giant container.

Followers of Christ seem to have come up with as many variations on the theme as there are fish in the sea. This could be viewed positively as well as negatively. And perhaps in the end it comes down to aesthetic components which may be entirely meaningless in the spiritual realm, no matter how seriously we take ourselves and our symbols.

Perhaps the historical diversity in Christian thought and practice can be compared to the ecosystem of a coral reef. There are times when, in an effort to promote the continued thriving of marine life, a suitable ship will be sunk as an artificial reef. Let us suppose this ship is the truth of Christ's death and resurrection as preserved in Scripture. It provides a basic structure upon which our spiritual reef can grow. In this scenario, diversity is the desired outcome. A thriving reef not only grows in size, but is also judged to be flourishing in direct relation to its variety. It is colorful, vibrant, and abundant. It has many levels of organism functioning effectively in specific individual roles. Soon it will completely envelope and transcend the ship which provided its basic structure to the extent that there will be no meaningful contact with it any longer. It has served its function, and though it remains deeply submerged and somewhat structurally relevant, the life of the reef carries on largely without it.

It makes for a winsome picture and one which many contemporary Christians perhaps unwittingly — or even wittingly — adhere to. There is no question that many followers of Christ consider Scripture essentially irrelevant. It did its job. It got things started. Look where we are now? Surely we do not need to be concerned about a thing sunken so far down in the cultural past we can barely even relate directly to it? We live on a flourishing reef with a life of its own. Our only real concern should be its continued flourishing.

But the reef is also full of predators and is subject to coral bleaching and other diseases. If it dies, what will remain? Scripture. That great structured wreck. That is the basis of our faith. Always has been. That is why the early Church adopted certain writings as Scripture. They describe the essence of the belief, passing it down to the rest of us so we can exist upon it. God can only be known through what He reveals. And Christ can only be known through what has been written.

Another imaginative approach to historical Christianity might be to compare it to — since we are on the fish theme — the glory of a monolithic creature such as the whale. Suppose the Body of believers in Christ is like that massive entity moving through the ocean of time. It changes, but is changeless. It moves, but is immovable. It adjusts to its environment without altering its essential nature. It is sublimely independent of cultural or political pressure in comparison to such a thing as a reef. It can swim wherever it likes the world over. It is a meta-cetacean, a sort of transcendent Christacean.

But it too, as glorious and free as it appears, is — like the coral reef — subject to disease and predation. And a beached whale is no good to anyone. No metaphor is perfect, but many are valid. Which will we choose? Perhaps neither. Or both. The larger point is, how should we as Christers live in this world in the absence of the Master's physical presence? As unified and transcendent fish? As coral polyps inhabiting a reified reef? How important are the differences between us? How meaningful? What are the essentials? How do we view the beliefs we claim to have? And how does that vision frame the world in which we live?

Let us return to the beginning of what has been called Christianity. There is no doubt that in the words of Christ, of Paul (Apostle of Christ), and most everyone else at the time, the advent of something big — even apocalyptic — seemed earth-shatteringly near. Indeed, some of this transcendent reality seemed to already have burst into being with Christ's life, death, and resurrection. Either the Kingdom of God in Christ's earthly ministry was manifesting shortly (if not already there), or the return of Christ was imminent in Paul's subsequent ministry. This is why, for instance, Paul encouraged singleness. Time was short. Why get married when Christ's return was just around the corner? Same with living in community and sharing all material goods. Why not? If the end was so near. This was not normative. It was not praxis. Nobody was building a religion. It was simply a logical response to the fast-approaching parousia (second coming of Christ) and/or apocalypse (end of times victory of good over evil), a practical no-brainer. The future was over. All plans were moot.

But then...Christ kept not coming back. The concluding present contained more future than anyone supposed. All the early followers died. How to keep the whale alive? How to promote the flourishing of the reef? Life began to settle into familiar patterns and routines. Human beings struggle to sustain faith in the absence of structures which have traditionally characterized belief. Such structures were subsequently built, institutions were formed, and creeds were hammered out. Social and financial bonds through marriage were once again promoted (except for the so-called priesthood). Family values and cultural conformity regained their age-old importance. Again, in effect, all of Christian history is simply an attempt to culturally modify faith in light of the ongoing non-return of Christ. And in this manner, two thousand years have gone by.

The argument could be made that, like the coral reef, all this edificial activity is a good thing, even edifying, the many isms and schisms a prismatic benefit to the multiform nature of the faith. Or...not. Perhaps it is all nonsense, just one damned (literally) thing after another, a sacerdotal costume party, Halloween every day, a clerical game of trick-or-treat.

For many who call themselves Christians, the current challenges of social, cultural, intellectual and technological complexity have become almost overwhelming. Perhaps it has always been this way. We are human. We are susceptible to the desire to simplify life in an effort to make it sustainable, even bearable.

So rather than accept and maintain complex and tiring individual distinctions of morality, and so-called Christian parameters of personal judgment, we easily fall prey to theological, teleological, ontological, and epistemological simplifications (or complications) which seem to offer livable solutions in each present historical moment. Comfort and safety are often mistakenly found in approved words and current ideas. How do we know something is a good idea? Good ideas work, and the best ideas work best. But what does it mean for something to work? Some ideas seem to work as intended, but have unintended long-term consequences. In this case they would ultimately be bad ideas. But such things can only be judged from an eternal perspective. Therefore, an eternal discernment must be brought to our day-to-day ideas. And this is only possible in light of a supernatural belief, for nature cannot give us the answers we seek. As the sages have said, a fish without fur says nothing about fur.

Some will say: if we do not understand God's wrath and eternal justice — and the personal responsibility this implies — let us rather simply say that God is love across all boundaries and behaviors, and that in the end all will be well, and all manner of things will be well. What a relief. And so easily done.

And if what we call "Scripture" is too complicated and too difficult to understand in its historical context, let us rather say that it is not Scripture at all, and therefore simply ignore it, or worse, use it as an old handbag jumbled full of potentially useful religious mottos, motifs, platitudes, mumbo-jumbo, claptrap, bric-a-brac, and whatnot with which we can add flavor to our lives without the benefit of any nutritive spiritual protein.

But the only way we can truly follow the Master — if that is in fact our confession — is to access the revelation we have, which is found in what we call Scripture. There is no other Christ available to us except in the realm of imagination.

It is no good crafting a simplification regarding Christ's meekness and non-judgmental love when the only actual reference we have shows him not to be exclusively behaving in such a manner. He is lovingly kind, yes, but also at times surprisingly — even disturbingly — harsh and judgmental. The red letters alone say it all, but some are more read than others, and some are not read at all. To believe Christ is only love and kindness is to be either fooling oneself, not reading the text, or not believing Christ's own words. Choose any of the three options. The outcome is inevitably one of fabricating a Christ who never existed. Life is not easy or simple, especially for followers of Christ. We must navigate depths and terrain far more extensive and intricate than those without faith, for we do not live in the shallows. Complexity is inescapable. Christ is both loving and judgmental, kind and harsh, sweet and salty.

The crux — a word meaning cross (how apropos) — is not to deny these diverse elements, but to consider how and why they are real, and consequently how to understand them in the context of our lives. Perhaps the truest route to spiritual simplicity is embracing revealed complexity rather than attempting to disregard difficulty. (Or by accepting the world's supposedly workable simplifications.)

So then: one could respond to the preceding parafabulon with a sense of despair, or hope, or even joy. After all, it is suggestive of our state. The Metafish was real. The experience was real. There is no doubt that something terrible and glorious befell the two fish, as it has we who follow the Master. We live in the radically ignorant middle ground — the my-called "fog of some-knowing" — between the events experienced by the two fish and the continued non-appearance of the Metafish.

Ours is a perpetual yearning, an active waiting, a restrained anticipation, this earth a home not home, a now not yet. We are hold-hovering the rescue helicopter, and it has been holding and hovering a long time. But then again, that is only a human perspective on time, for "one day is with the Lord as a thousand years, and a thousand years as one day".[9]

These metaphorical musings bring to mind the story told of a group of ancient travelers whose narrow route through the mountains was blocked fore and aft by massive rockslides. They were stuck in that high place so long life itself became the stoppage. Or rather, the stoppage itself became life. They built shelters, terraced and farmed hillsides, begat children and grandchildren. In time their point of departure, their original destination, and the reason for their journey in the first place, all faded into the realm of myth, into legends and fables told around the campfire generation after generation. When the way forward to their promised land was finally cleared from the other side, they had no desire to go anywhere, for they had become moderately comfortable and could not muster the courage or desire to undergo the discomfort and hardship required for that final push into their destiny.

Let us not be them. Born again, this is our native home no more. Human flourishing is not our telos. Spiritual nourishing is. But we will take shalom wherever we can get it, and give it out on every side, keeping in mind that results most often modify downwards. The best chance at an earthly shalom is the pursuit of a heavenly peace, for to insist upon an earthly heaven is to all but guarantee a mortal hell. Human flourishing — like happiness — is a byproduct of a meaningful life, and what more proliferant meaning could there be than the highest ideal, which is Christ? For fish — and those who fish — what could possibly be better than a Metafish? Well, nothing that I can think of, for if we hunger, we will eat, and if we eat, we will live, and if we live, we will surely not die.

Therefore, be of proportionate significance to one's circumstance. For the Master is not a concierge, planning our every excursion into the world at our every whim. We have his map. We have our minds. We have his Spirit. Let us swim as we must — even if it is against the current — and grow as we are grown.

Let us take up our individual responsibilities as a backpack, or even a cross. For the Master is also not a bellhop. There are times when we must manage the stairs ourselves and perhaps even abandon our extraneous luggage, for baggage claim is only for those determined to burden themselves with such possessions. His yoke is easy, and his burden light.[10] Why make it heavy?

If he is our Metafish, we are free. We can not only stand fast in him, but also move fast in his power. For time is no longer our enemy, but the content of our ocean.

And the ocean of time is limitless, as is the contentment of our souls. For ours is not a slough of despond,[11] but rather a rich, multivariate marsh of ultimate conservation.

In it we swim beyond our limits, still and forever within the eternal bounds — and self-adjustable bonds — of everlasting meaning.

Pause and consider.

CHAPTER 2

DOG

PARAFABULON #1

Once there was a dog who lived in the dust of the street, caught rats and did whatever he wanted. He was often hungry, always thirsty, and forever dirty.

A stranger appeared unto him one day as he was panting in the shade, avoiding the noonday sun.

"You are a dog and your life is hard," said the stranger.

"Yes," said the dog, watching the stranger carefully.

"I will tell you a secret that will change your life forever," said the stranger.

"What is this secret?" said the dog.

"It is very simple, but very powerful," said the stranger.

"Will it make me clean, put food in my belly, and water in my mouth?" said the dog, for he imagined all this could be a good thing. Indeed, he could dream of nothing better.

"Only do this thing, and what you have wished for will come

true," said the stranger.

"Tell me, and I will do it," said the dog.

"You must learn to walk on your two hind legs," said the stranger.

This made the dog sad, for he had always walked on four legs and it was not in his nature to walk on two legs.

"I cannot walk on two legs," said the dog, looking down into the dust between his front paws.

"No," said the stranger. "Not yet, and not without effort. Even a human baby must crawl before it can walk."

"It sounds complicated," said the dog.

"On the contrary," said the stranger, "it is very simple. But it is also very hard."

When the dog looked up, the stranger was gone, and was soon forgotten.

But the dog's life became even bleaker as the days passed, and he began to feel the nearness of death. Then he remembered what the stranger had said.

"I have nothing to lose," the dog thought to himself. "I must try the stranger's secret, for I do believe what he suggested must be possible."

It was very difficult to do what the stranger had said, but in the believing, and in the doing, the dog did learn to walk on two legs. And everything the stranger said did come true. He was given food and water, as much as he could swallow. He was taken in and clipped and cleaned, as clipped and clean as any dog could hope to be. His life was changed completely.

"I must tell other dogs this secret," he thought, and he did so. Many dogs were changed in this manner.

But time passed and the dog grew tired of walking on two legs, for it still was not natural and required a constant effort. There came moments when he would secretly drop to all fours once again, just for a short time. But these times became more frequent and he eventually found himself back in the dust of the street, catching rats and thirsting after water.

The day came when he felt a darkness unrelated to the sun closing in upon him as he lay panting in the shade. A voice came unto him saying, "What was the secret of the good life?"

"I will tell you," said the dog, and he shared again the secret of walking on two legs.

There was a long silence and the voice said, "Why therefore are you dirty and hungry and thirsty?"

"Oh, I am not really dirty and hungry and thirsty, for I can walk on two legs at any time."

And he immediately died in the dust of the street.

PARAFABULON #2

Once upon a time there were two dogs lying in a manger. They did not eat any of the grain therein themselves and yet they would not allow any other animal to eat the grain or use the manger. The two dogs would bark, and bare their teeth, and all the animals called them awful, selfish, and rude. All the people thereabouts were afraid of them also. Not a one — human or animal — had a good word to say about them.

"May I graze upon it?" said the cow.

"No!" said the dogs.

"May I nibble on it?" said the sheep.

"No!" said the dogs.

"May I peck at it?" said the chicken.

"No!" said the dogs.

One day an angel from heaven appeared before them.

"May I sleep upon it?" said the angel.

"No!" said the dogs.

Not long after this, a young couple arrived with a baby.

"May we use the manger for our baby?" said the couple. "We have nowhere else to go."

The dogs made not a sound. They left the manger and went on their way.

The years passed in typical ancient dog fashion. The two dogs survived as best they could, roaming from town to town, scavenging any morsel of food they could find.

It came to pass that on the outskirts of a town, as the two dogs were escaping the heat of the noonday sun under a bush, they saw a rich man amble along the road, just in front of their noses. They followed him at a distance.

"He may drop crumbs," said the one dog.

"We will eat them," said the other.

But the rich man did not drop crumbs. He did not even help a poor man who was lying on the side of the road, covered in sores.

The two dogs licked the poor man's sores, which brought the poor man some measure of relief. But a crowd of passersby were revolted by this sight and threw stones in their direction, chasing them off.

"Bad dogs!" they said.

It came to pass that one day the two dogs were on a hill. There were crowds of people surging this way and that, and a number of men were nailed to crosspieces of wood which stood up out of the ground. The two dogs were drawn to one of these men. Blood ran from him his side and there was a crown of thorns upon his head.

The man saw the two dogs as they drew near and said unto them, "I cannot offer you anything beyond what you have already been given."

The dogs wagged their tails gently.

"We never expected anything but this," they said, "for we are only dogs."

"Good dogs," said the man.

RUMINATIO

Dogs are harbingers. What is a harbinger? It is a breed of omen. What is an omen? Something we hope is good and does not bite us on the providence. And as dogs fetch thrown sticks from field-side bushes, so their trope may also retrieve meaning from the concealing cultural foliage, for metaphor is strong with them.

However, as amusing as it is to encourage such canine-related imagery to romp and frolic, it is important to remember that dogs are primarily animals. Some will bark, some will bite, and some will do both. And some will do neither. When it comes to dogs, it is the master that matters.

Many dog owners believe personal fondness for their pet surely propagates across all social and interpersonal boundaries. This presumption is unfounded. Like faith, one man's precious dog is another man's pesky mongrel. Faith only makes sense to the faithful and, well, sometimes a little training and discipline makes for a more useful furry disciple than a woolly beast roaming untethered. What I am trying to say is, we must keep our faith on a leash. It does not need to go around yapping and biting people.

Dogs have an ambiguous interpretive pedigree. The good, the bad, and the muttly (so to speak), for there is the potential for bad and good — and a mixed breed of both — in every one of us. Therefore, two parafabula for this chapter seems apropos. After all, does not the Master have the right to make of one lump of fur one dog for one purpose and one for another? And we too have the mind of the Master.

Consider then the metaphorical dog in its negative connotation. We have all heard the prophetic phrase, "going to the dogs". It could be civilization, the neighborhood, a career, one's house — even conceivably one's dog could be going to the dogs. This phrase is the symbolic epitome of failure, collapse, deterioration, and even moral degeneration.

But consider also the metaphorical dog in its positive capacity. Consider the canine concept of the dog as "man's best friend". It is then the very personification of faithfulness, trustworthiness, servanthood, companionship, even friendship.

And how do we mortals compare? Jesus himself called us dogs, referring to most of us.[12] And as far as the Scriptures are concerned, definitely not using the positive motif. One hungrily wanders the wordsy avenues of the Bible like a stray dog, searching in vain for even the tiniest metaphorical morsel affirming dogness. Jews — of whom Christ was one — viewed dogs as possibly the lowest of predatory pack animals. Scavengers. Vultures of the canine world. Even dead bodies were unsafe from their unclean foraging. They were not individualized or personalized as pets. They were a pack. But let us unpack this Christic canine classification.

For Christ, Jews were metaphorically sheep (part of the fold) and gentiles were dogs (not part of the fold). He came for the sheep because he was their Shepherd, a Jew himself, their Messiah.[13] Many of his sheep he referred to as lost.[14] A shepherd does not search for stray dogs, but gathers his sheep. Dogs, in this case, are simply a nuisance and an interference. Maybe even a threat. And certainly food for the sheep would not be shared with the dogs.

Christ came to earth, in his own words, as the Jewish Messiah. But he was not at all what the majority were expecting. They tried to get rid of him. They got rid of him.

But good news — he came right back from death to life. And his sheep, did they recognize him? No, they did not. At least, not many. Good news again, at least from the perspective of we negative dog types, for the world is full of gentiles. The dogs not only got crumbs falling from the Master's table, they were invited to share the children's bread itself. In fact, they were given a place at the Master's very table. Is it any wonder that dogs are portrayed in art as playing poker, after such a big win as this? We dogs have all become sons and daughters if we are in Christ. Not bad for an upgrade. Rags to riches; wags to ichthys. (So to speak.)

This is an age of God's grace being poured out upon the earth. One may call it a dispensational deluge or even the opening of a heavenly pharmakon. God's faith pharmacy dispensing grace free of charge, all expenses paid under the salvation plan, and no fees on the prescription. This distributive trope is at times hard to understand or render convincingly, even when employing more conventional wording. Many are covenantally confused. We forget our true dogness, opting instead for taming dogmas. We mistake Christ's words to his sheep as applying to us dogs. Christ clearly states they do not. Context is everything. Christ has become our Savior only as a result of his rejection by those he came for. But there may be a future for them yet. As sheep. This is a topic for another time and place. I myself have trouble enough of my own, though I possess neither dogs nor sheep.

However, it should be said, the apostle renamed Paul, inspired by Christ — if one cares to read about it — is very clear about some of these matters. We are living in a special time, a spiritual time, a graceful time. It is easy to take for granted. And easy to forget how it all came about. Only ask the question — what if Jesus Christ had been accepted by his sheep, the Children of Israel? What if he had not been crucified? And what if he had not subsequently risen from the dead? Pause and consider.

This world is as real as we can endure in our current form. It is not primary or final; it is only mediate. And so are we. It is a dog's breakfast, that is for sure. (Not the same dog's breakfast I mentioned previously in the Preface, for not all meals are the same.) A bit of a mess. But perhaps one day we will — as the scholars like to say — blow this hot dog stand, for indeed, things are going to get hot for many a dog, and a horn will blow. Who will then stand?

If this then is true, how are we to live? What is it we are actually trying to do as followers of Christ on this earth? Well, nothing. And everything. That is, the earth itself is not our primary focus. Christ — and our spiritual life in Him — is. But such transcendent logic will inform our secondary actions within this present arena more surely, clearly, and personally than any worldly mission statement or global commissional goal. For we are heavenly beings blooming in earthly fields; we are well-planted wheat; we are compliant canines. We are the obedient every-dog to the merciful only-Master, awaiting his will. And if every dog has its day, then this is our day.

This, of course, does not reduce our responsibility. Indeed, it is maximized, for we are operating from the perspective of eternity. There is no avoiding it: our Being itself in this fluid habitat must supernaturally effervesce. And such unearthly fizzing and bubbling will naturally result in earthly consequence, for even as kindred spirits rise in carbonated sympathy, we, like any good plant capable of fixing nitrogen from the air to the enrichment of the soil, will also fix unseen, immeasurable good from the transcendent atmosphere to the betterment of this earth.

I have recently become aware via electronic media of a concept called "otherkin". In an extension of ongoing developments in gender ideology, it is the idea that one can conceive of oneself as a type of animal — or even mythical creature — trapped within a human body. I will not ridicule the concept here. That may well come later, though it is hardly necessary, for the idea quite sufficiently mocks itself. However, taking a cue and some inspiration from such creative conceptualizations, one could prophetically say we Christers are "Christ-Beings" — "Notherkin", to coin a word — currently situated within these human bodies. (I am under no illusion the neologistic "Notherkin" will ever enter common usage, though I would be happy to be de-disillusioned of such a non-delusion.) But we Notherkin do not require any special acknowledgment, for one of the main characteristics of being Notherkin is lowliness and sacrifice. We require nothing, for we are dead to ourselves, and the dead, of course, also require nothing. Our "recognition" attains from a higher metaphysical realm.

So then: we Christers are the Notherkin. We are human, but other. That is, Nother. We are not types of animals (otherkin) trapped in human bodies, we are spiritual creatures flourishing in human form. For this moment in our development, we are situated in these "material" bodies, like an image in a projector, but we also exist in a sort of spiritual entanglement on an alternate plane where only those who follow Christ exist. In the spiritual world we do not occupy the same structure as those who do not follow Christ. The question is, how does this affect our interactions in these bodies in the present world — in this space and at this time? All Notherkin have shoulders, and therefore must shoulder the responsibilities and mode of conduct proper to the Notherkin's physical form in this space and time, according to the will of the Master.

Christerica, more than anything, is a mode of being conducted in light of a transcendent reality adopted by faith. We are literally performers, enacting given roles regardless of fugitive tendencies. We act as we should, not because we want to or are even good at it, but because it is the right thing to do in context of the narrative we follow. We are actors following a script we believe is true, or at least true as anything we are apt to encounter in this life. For Christ is our scriptwriter, our Holy Ghostwriter, assigning responsibility to immediate concerns, both spiritual and physical. Not for the sake of endless human flourishing or the redemption of the earth, but for the sake of holiness and the sanctification required for numinous realities. Indeed, we are simply responsible for our responsibilities. Our mortal lives are not to be used as opportunities for self-actualization, but rather as mantles of responsibility in keeping with a higher reality whose portal of entry is Christ.

In a sense, we must imagine the earth as a sort of rental property we inhabit but do not own. And as followers of Christ, we care for that rental property, not because of any self-serving notion that some day we might own it — or at the least be awarded parcels of land as portions of some inheritance — but because it is simply the right and responsible thing to do.

As a child, my family lived in many different places, primarily in South America. My parents' approach to every circumstance was the same: we should leave that place in better condition than when we arrived. That was our responsibility. We must act similarly towards our physical bodies. We care for them and treat them as a God-given responsibility in Christ, not for our own pleasure or subsequent short-term flourishing, but because it is the right thing to do. For at the very least, there should be some discomfort with comfort, some unease with ease, some discontentment with contentment, some displeasure with pleasure, some dissatisfaction with satisfaction, some offence at affluence, some...well, one gets the idea.

A belief in a truncated, earthly view of our faith invariably leads to heresy and idolatry, to mortal obsessions with power and politics, and quasi-romantic entanglements with personal rights and public entitlements. We cannot help ourselves. Like a dog returning to its vomit, we find it hard to resist the attractions of our ancient disease, pride, that great sin. We should expect nothing, for false expectations are the breeding ground of disappointment, and we are not of that breed. Entitlement is a cancer. Expect nothing and you will not only be free, but grateful for everything.

Paul tells the believers in Thessalonica they should study — or make it their aim or ambition — to lead a tranquil life, work with their hands, and mind their own business.[15]

And why not? Why could this not be a commission? Love

each other and make it our goal to live a quiet life. To mind our own business. To not be a burden to others, as much as it is in our power.

Simple. Humble. Holy. And entirely doable. (Though not easy.)

Not everything is large. Most things are small. And most large things are just small things combined. And dogs come in many sizes, as do we.

Maybe we are not here to "save the world", so to speak, but to assist — like every good service dog — in freeing (and guiding) minds and spirits, and to promote the living of quiet lives, the trusting in Christ, the living morally, and the growing in spiritual maturity. Love, joy, peace, patience, kindness, goodness, faithfulness, gentleness, and self-control. No law against any of these.[16]

A focus on earthly power, material wealth, political control, sexual politics, and so on, is in some sense a denial of our reality as spiritual beings who already at this moment occupy a responsible position in the heavenlies. Our mortal orientations and desires must be subsumed under the greater spiritual reality in which we exist, and what that requires of our perishable bodies. The perishable does not dictate the imperishable. Does a bone choose a dog? Not that I am aware of. The tail does not wag the dog, but if it does, the dog is in for a very strange life.

Can this be difficult? Of course. We all have our challenges.

But what else can it mean to take up our cross and follow Christ? Who would expect anything less? We so often pray to be used by God, then call it abuse and betrayal when that prayer is answered. We must crucify any dream or desire which does not promote our spiritual growth in Christ. And try to carry each other's burdens.

We are severely limited. As Paul himself says, we see through a glass darkly.[17] Who could argue with that? We are flesh and blood, meat and bone. As dogs we can do almost nothing, but we must do the little we can. After all, we have the perfect Master, if only we will listen to him and obey his voice, a voice that continues to call us friends and companions as we train our spiritual noses to the scent, tracking him upon this our narrow path through life.

Seek and ye shall find, yes, but once the Master is found, seek no longer, but follow and live. For a seeker constantly seeking is as lost as a dog straying from home.

May our shaggy hides be blessed. May our redeemed tails wag freely. May our heavenly homing instinct be supremely honed.

Paws and consider.

CHAPTER 3

CAT

<u>PARAFABULON</u>

There once was a curious cat who climbed into a box. The lid of the box closed over it and the cat was not able to get out.

"I am trapped," thought the cat. "I should have not been so curious."

In a corner of the box was a strange contraption which — unknown to the cat — was potentially deadly.

The cat, whose eyes had now adjusted to the darkness, looked at the contraption.

"I wonder what is that," thought the cat. She reached out a paw towards it, but then remembered how curiosity had trapped her in the box in the first place.

So she tucked her feet under her and waited patiently, looking at it. She tried to think.

Her thoughts were like mice which vanished as soon as she bit their tail.

"What will I do," she thought, "when my thoughts are like

mice I cannot catch?"

Time passed, and the cat's master, who had been searching for her high and low, had only one place left to look.

"I know and fear that she must be in the box with the potentially deadly contraption," he said. "Therefore, she will be both dead and alive until I look. And so, I will not look, for if I look she may be dead, and if I do not look she may be alive."

Soon, though, a new thought came to him.

"However," he thought, "without food and water, she will surely die, whether I look or not."

At this, he immediately lifted the lid of the box.

But the cat was not there.

RUMINATIO

When Erwin Schrödinger first postulated the now-famous thought experiment involving the cat in the box, he meant the example as a critique of the existing view of quantum mechanics. Instead it became the very touchstone for the proponents of that view. History is funny that way.

Søren Kierkegaard sacrificed a lifetime of money, energy, inwardness, and literary genius — not to mention marital bliss

— in developing the pivotal role of the subjective individual in response to God's truth in the existence of Christ. History remembers him as one of the founders of existentialism, a generally Godless philosophical position very few would suspect relates to Christ at all.

Such is life. Baffling. Perplexing. Inexplicable in its shifting moods and mysterious manifestations. Like a cat. Like the Holy Spirit. Is that too abrupt a lateral leap? Well, it illustrates my point perfectly. Who has not been startled and confounded by the sudden movements of a cat or the astonishing interventions of the Holy Spirit? The real surprise in either case would be predictability.

Cats indeed seem emblematic of the Holy Spirit. There is no Scripture to warrant this. I am just saying. The Bible hardly mentions cats at all, despite historical exposure to the well-known Egyptian cat worship and general Egyptian feline familiarity. Or perhaps that is precisely why the Jews stayed clear of them. They left the flesh-pots of Egypt — and its emblematic cats — behind. And good riddance.

Two of the most common representations of the Holy Spirit in Scripture are fire[18] and wind.[19] Neither of which are exactly representations per se, but really sort of unpredictable and unmanageable forces subject to invisible and unforeseeable powers. They come and go as they please. They carry their potential for destruction very close to the surface. They rush and jump. They appear and disappear. They…well, they start to remind one of a cat.

Why did Schrödinger choose a cat? Does it matter? We now have it. Perhaps that is enough. It is the perfect animal for such a thing. Cats are like that. Who knows what they are up to? Who knows which way they will jump? They are curious, but they are careful too. Everyone has heard of a "scaredy-cat". Chances are if we put one in a box it would not wreck everything right away, but might just sit there, looking around in the dark. Or not. All cats are grey at night.

In any case, as a consequence of Schrödinger's creative fancy, we now have a term which is useful on many levels. This term is "cat states", really just another name for a paradox. A cat state is a situation where — like Schrödinger's cat in the box — a thing can be in two states (dead or alive, for example) at the same time until by observation it collapses (decoherence) into one state or the other. This is also called "superposition". Cat states are an integral part of the world of quantum physics, and not just in an abstract or theoretical sense. There are real-world applications: like lasers; and computer hard drives; then there's quantum computing. None of which I know anything about. This is a book of parafabula, not a science paper, thanks be to God.

I am simply interested in the concept of cat states as an interpretive scratching post upon which to exercise some ideas regarding Christerica and the life of the Spirit. Quantum entanglement is to theology what cat states are to pneumatology. If only I knew what that meant.

Cat states proliferate in the Christian realm. For instance,

Scripture is both authoritative and interpretive at the same time. Christ is both God and man at the same time. God is present and not-present at the same time. God speaks and is silent at the same time. Then there is free will and determinism, love and wrath, forgiveness and judgment. Cat states everywhere.

In the life of the Spirit, we must resist interpretive decoherence. The dynamic dualism of Christerical cat states are real functions. We each of us have real value in its domain. Everything is in a radical state of catness, so to speak. Stable, but multivalent. Only God looks in the box. Only the Spirit of God collapses the wave function. Cat states are in fact God states. We live in tension.

Some theorize that everything we perceive as material reality is in fact fundamentally structured vibration. The geometric forms produced by these oscillating forces manifest as objects to our senses. Perhaps everything in the universe — everything material and immaterial alike — is just information given shape. I have said this before and may say it again: every human artifact is an idea given shape, an idea imposed upon the "natural" world. (A world, one might add, given to entropy.) The natural world is in some sense alive. To implement our ideas, we must eliminate whatever life force is inherent in the material in order to shape it to our ideas of design and permanence. But everything we make is also subject to entropy. In time, nature reclaims its dead material from our built structures — and our very bodies — digesting them entropically for continued use in its ongoing life cycle.

So then, what is life? What are these ideas we keep having, and where do they come from? They are not natural, for nature has no ideas. Therefore they are by definition supernatural. But what is this supernatural, this reality whose primary evidence is the ideas we impose upon the natural world? No wonder the Bible says God spoke everything into existence. Speech propagates as invisible wave patterns which we perceive as meaning. They are shaped to our senses and our senses are shaped in return.

Of course, it depends who is talking. Speaking is not always communication. One person's nonsense is another's wisdom. How do we discern something as abstract as truth? It seems the life of the spirit is often a matter of more delicate instrumentation, of being attuned to higher registers. Perhaps this is why silence is so crucial. We must speak less and say more. We must not only hear, but hear well. How else to perceive these subtle signals?

But I would like to say a thing or two about purring. What are cats up to? There is frequency. There is vibration. But is it communication? Or is it something else? Nobody knows. It is a mystery. Perhaps we could even call it a cat state, for it is most likely not just one thing for one purpose, but multiple things simultaneously.

Therapeutic ultrasound has been in use for some time in the service of promoting healing in tissue and bone. I am told its benefits are mainly due to increased blood flow to the treatment area.

But I am no physician. I simply want to talk about cats. And there is some suggestion that purring, by its vibrational nature, may accomplish in cats something similar to what ultrasound accomplishes in humans. This may even be part of the reason why cats recover so well from physical trauma, leading to the legend of their nine lives.

But I am no veterinarian. I simply want to talk about the Holy Spirit. (And need I list the nine-fold fruit of the Spirit again in this respect? I think not. The connection is obvious.) There is some suggestion that God's ability to shape reality is so vibrationally complex it can promote healing at levels of effectiveness even purring and ultrasound cannot reach. We might call this a miracle. But miracle is just a word for an effect we do not comprehend.

Imagine if one had the ability to perceive the universe vibrationally. Surely angels have such ability. (Though I have a hunch they cannot sing or make music as well as we mortals.) They exist in a different vibrational state. Perhaps visible to cats. Is this what cats seem to be looking at? Is this why they run manically to and fro? One day we will surely know as we are known.

What we call higher beings are simply beings of higher vibrational complexity. Beings invisible to us due to the limited sensory capabilities we possess. At the highest level God is not only able to view the entire spectrum of reality, but also able to manipulate it. Perhaps in the vast transcendental tapestry of this universe, we appear to Him as nodes of vibrational effect within that great invisible warp and weft. Our individuality is embedded. To be perfectly tuned beings we must be in humble harmony with not only our world, but the entire universe. The Holy Spirit is the tuning agent. And no wonder we do not always comprehend the Holy Spirit's working. If we are out of tune, how can we possibly know it except by the intervention of a Higher Tuner?

If we could see what God sees, if we could see the way Christ sees, we could perhaps discern in each other supernatural beauty in terms of perfect vibrational humility. What we mortals actually see is only a rough material representation of underlying potential in regards to the all-encompassing nodal network. (More on that later in connection with webs and spiders, or spiders and webs, however one likes to put it.) No wonder we are instructed not to be respecters of persons. We are metaphysical beings.

The crucial factor is to seek to understand one's own unique modality and nodality, allowing the current of the Spirit to flow freely through the network at one's node and in the manner of one's node. In a way, we are like faucets. Who gives credit to a faucet? Nobody. One simply activates the tap and water pours through. But the more freely the Pure water flows, the cleaner and more useful the faucet becomes. The best faucet is the faucet most willing to be a faucet. This is humility on tap. A well-tuned soul is one perfectly attuned to the Holy Spirit in one's full vibrational circumstance.

I once saw a movie called "The Matrix". The main character

— Neo — did not realize he was living in a computer simulation. Another character — Morpheus — offered him the choice between a blue pill perpetuating the illusory status quo, and a red pill revealing "the truth" behind apparent reality. We are all — or have been — in Neo's position. A Christer is simply one who has been truly "red-pilled", for Christ himself is the red pill, a life-saving capsule whose dispensation supplies the life-altering antidote of his blood given against the enchanted blindness of our natural condition. The veil is lifted, for, as Morpheus says to Neo, "All I am offering is the truth." And once you have ingested Christ, that truth is indeed revealed.

The Holy Spirit of God is immaterial. It moves like the wind, and like the wind, blows wherever it wills. Indeed, the very shape of the Christer's invisible form is sculpted by the winds of the Spirit. It cannot be contained or controlled by mere mortals. It cannot be tamed or used. Like a cat, it must be allowed to approach, it must be given space, proper reception and perception. It must be given attention and silence. In a lifetime of silence and contemplation, one may never literally sense God in any apprehensible form, never hear His voice, never see His presence. And yet, at the exact same time, that same silence may be profoundly generative, and one may be left with the impression of a Presence continually streaming subconscious data through one, and through everything around one. And everything around one, through and through — trees, animals, waves, wind, flowers, loved ones and so on — may seem completely saturated with that same Presence.

Like the sky, there is no blue in it, and yet it is blue, overwhelmingly.

We are all in need of constant metaphysical therapy. Sound and silence are in superposition, a cat state if ever there was one. There is real value at every level of potential measurement, whether measured or not. Christ alone, operating at the quantum level, evaluates this counterfactual definiteness and through the Holy Spirit, applies.

The Spirit — like a cat, like the wind, like fire — moves in mysterious ways. And only an empty heart can be filled, for only an empty heart has room for the Spirit of God.

But such is a cat — it comes to those who wait. And who are silent. And who are still.

And so the Holy Spirit.

Pause and consider.

CHAPTER 4

COW

<u>PARAFABULON</u>

A calf stood in a large field. It saw a high pasture upon a nearby mountain.

"The green in that place looks nice," said the calf. "If I could get there, I would go there."

The old bull overheard this and said, "There is a narrow passage. You will find it between two large rocks just past the stream at the base of the mountain."

The calf immediately went and found the hidden passage.

"I would never have found this on my own," said the calf, as she followed the narrow passage.

The high pasture was as fresh and green as she had imagined. And there was also a spring of fresh water.

The calf went there every day — day after day — as the sun tumbled up into the sky, and the grass grew ever longer and the water ever fresher. It was her favorite place.

But then — she did not know why — she forgot about it. It

simply left her mind. There were other things to do and see, see and do.

And then something even stranger happened, and it happened to her. It was time, more than the usual amount. Time had somehow marinated her flesh and bone with such thorough saturation that she had not only been transformed into a full-grown cow, but — and this may not be believed — it had penetrated her so deeply and grown so much extra cow that she actually produced another separate cow, a small one, from within herself.

And there came a day when her calf saw the high pasture and desired it.

"We will go to the high green," said the cow, "I will show you."

But the passage was now too narrow for her and she could not get through. This troubled her greatly.

"What will I do?" she thought. "I will ask the wise old bull."

And so she did.

The old bull said, "There is only one way for one of such time dimensions to gain the high pasture."

"What is this way?" said the cow.

"You must become a calf again."

"How is this possible?" said the cow.

The old bull slanted a head and rubbed a horn against a tree.

"I have literally no idea," he said.

RUMINATIO

What is the meaning of life?

The meaning of life is the solution to death. What else could it possibly be? Any other meaning falls short of our ultimate need. Survival alone is not meaning enough, for it is only temporary. Survival is only fending off nature until we are annihilated by time. Life's events only take on meaning in light of some higher purpose which transcends death. Meaning is a light source which only shines under external power.

But what then is the solution to death? Well that would be the meaning of life. So let us search out the answer together. That is, both the meaning and the solution, which are potentially one and the same.

As we can see from this chapter's parafabulon, partial answers are not always workable solutions, and though cattle may be far more interpretively useful than previously considered, they may still place us upon the horns of a dilemma. A key, after all, is only functional in the correct configuration. What of a key wrongly cut? It must be transformed by the renewing of its grind. Sometimes what to do and how to do it seem irredeemably isolated. Can the separation be bridged or, even better yet, eliminated? Can it be — dare I say it — redeemed? Indeed, can a corniform conundrum become a horn of plenty?

What doesn't kill you, makes you stronger — or simply damages you beyond repair. But the gnarled trunk of an ancient tree is testament to its bounteous life. Do not despair. One's life is a grave task, for life's task is one's grave. One is steadily building one's own mausoleum, for one will inescapably be buried in this inevitable monument to one's existence. Who will free us from this tomb? Who will crack this catacomb? Who will decrypt this crypt? Well, of course, that transcendent Robin Hood of graves, our Master Christ. For he robs from the niche and gives to the pore, every bit of his being a bite of freedom betokening a heavenly banqueting table.

Ponder this: what if we knew we had a year to live? What would we do? How would we live? Would we change anything? No? Yes? Think of it as a diagnostic tool of sorts. Whatever changes we might envision could be a sign of cognitive dissonance or even spiritual imbalance. There are a few ways to look at this. It is not totally unambiguous that discrepancy alone is negative. It could be a sign we are living our life responsibly despite yearnings and desires kept in check by moral maturity or a proper regard for those under our care. Or it could be a sign we are not living our life well at all, but simply miscalculating the requirements and possibilities of our condition as we chart our progress through time and space.

Are we responsible but frustrated? Irresponsible but idealistic? Whatever the case may be, it would seem the ideal to strive for would be to look to the highest ethic and meaning possible while simultaneously being transformed in such way that our actions would reflect that higher ethic perfectly. Can this be done? Yes, if we were cattle. But as humans, the best we can hope for is to see our ideals manifested in some practical way in our lives as lived, not only for our benefit but for the benefit of every one and every thing affected by our active being.

The Christer formulation mentioned in the Preface helps to promote this lifestyle integrity. If Christing is a verb, then in Christ, we Christ. If our goal is to Christ, then Christing is our life. If I am Christing now, I will be Christing tomorrow, the day after, and a year from now. No difference. Christing all the way, 24/7. And death? To live is Christ, to die is gain.[20] If the meaning of life is Christing, then the solution to death is Christing as well. Christing transcends this world, persisting into eternity, for Christ is eternal.

There is something childlike and innocent in the simplicity of this idea. If the only way to reach the high pasture in the parafabulon is to become a calf again, then perhaps we are on the right track. Christ himself told his disciples they must become like little children to enter the kingdom of heaven.[21] Indeed, we must be born again to participate in the Body of Christ.[22] Perhaps too there is something childlike in the nature of God Himself.

I have always been intrigued by this passage from G.K.

Chesterton's book *Orthodoxy*:

Because children have abounding vitality, because they are in spirit fierce and free, therefore they want things repeated and unchanged. They always say, "Do it again"; and the grown-up person does it again until he is nearly dead. For grown-up people are not strong enough to exult in monotony. But perhaps God is strong enough to exult in monotony. It is possible that God says every morning, "Do it again" to the sun; and every evening, "Do it again" to the moon. It may not be automatic necessity that makes all daisies alike; it may be that God makes every daisy separately, but has never got tired of making them. It may be that he has the eternal appetite of infancy; for we have sinned and grown old, and our Father is younger than we.[23]

Is it not true? We grow old. God does not. What if God really is a "childlike God"? Not childish, but child-like. Events throughout the Bible may take on a fresh perspective through such a lens. God delights in untrammelled play, in outrageous acts of creation and imagination. He loves coincidence. He loves repetition. He loves serendipity, but also consistency. He loves the things He has made. He is a righteous God, a jealous God. He delights in youthful faith. He loves honesty and hates deceit. His wrath descends upon the immoral, the cruel, and the hardened. He hates sin. He hates haters. He hates people wrecking His stuff.

Perhaps this is what many of us do not understand about God. He is young. Young in the sense that He is not old. If time for

Him does not exist, then age does not exist for Him either. He is outside of time. His angels as well. If He likes something, as Chesterton suggests, then He likes it forever and ever. Because our forever and ever is simply His eternal present. Why must we be born again to be Christers? Well, to become God-like little children. To trust and believe with the simplicity of a child. To have that same humility and sincerity.

Perhaps God is both incredibly wise and eternally childlike at the same time. (Another "cat state", if one has read the last chapter.) It is always the new believer in whom God rejoices. He loves the pure in heart. To see an old person with the heart of a child is almost a miracle. Age can do terrible things to the human heart. Time may heal wounds, as they say, but it can be hell on faith.

Consider various characters in the Bible: Moses, Samson, David, Solomon. Heroes get old. And if their faith gets old, what then? It is a sad and terrible thing. Faith ages only by changing. And it changes by following the world and the sinful human heart. Pause and consider: heaven does not change. The world of the spirit does not change. God does not change.

In the Biblical narrative, it is Lucifer — the light-bringer — who aged spiritually, becoming the adversary we now call Satan, using whatever small amount of light he retains to mesmerize the unwary like a remorseless deep-sea predator with its attractive — but ultimately deadly — phosphorescence. Why else would he think he knew better than a childlike God? And some of the angels — they got old, too. No longer was it simply enough to contemplate the everlasting glory of the Creator, for the high pasture is only accessible to the young at heart. The fatted cow can only observe from afar, no longer able to graze upon such distant delights. No wonder our parafabulous old bull could only rub a horn against a tree and plead ignorance to the cow's query, for we all know from whence came the calf. And what more can a wise old bull do, but give limited advice and germinate new life?

I once saw a child laughing and crying at the same time, and immediately the thought of God came to my mind. For surely God laughs and cries in the same way over every saved and lost soul, the joy and pain are so great. We cannot do justice to this enormity. It beggars the mind. Imagine then God in Christ, with these monumental childlike sensibilities — never mind his True nature — enduring what he endured. How glib we are to take it for granted. How easily we think we know better. How quickly we scoff at the spiritual wonders we marvelled at in our youth. Age alone can do that, as indeed many who read this paragraph will prove by examining their private thoughts.

So then: if I am taking life too seriously, perhaps I am not taking it seriously enough. True Christerical seriousness has more than a touch of comedy. Seriously. We must forget about ourselves. We are not so great. If there is greatness, it is in Christ. No amount of human seriousness will save a lost soul. Nor will it glorify the follower of Christ. Of course, I am talking about joy. But who knows anything about joy? We all just want to be happy. And maybe that is our problem.

In cow terms, if we graze upon Christ, we will graze upon Christ forever, calf to cow, cow to heavenly pasture. To graze is to live. And, as far as cows go, it should be mentioned that cows share one thing, and share it uncommonly well. That is cow-ness. Very rarely is a cow mistaken for anything else, in either form or character. This stability of nature — this spiritual coherence and solidarity — is much to be admired.

A similarly visible unity in diversity should in some way characterize Christerica. But how can we be One in Christ if we perpetuate difference in the cause of faith? If we politicize and bureaucratize the Christer life? The only way we can be one is to eliminate ritual as a defining element. Sacred cows only serve to cow the sacred. And we are the sacred if we are in Christ. This is why Christ says we must worship in spirit and in truth. Churchianity has been used as a word to describe the legalistic nature and overt focus on externals which has characterized much of historical Christianity. It is a fitting word. Rules, rituals, and regulations seem to be the inevitable religious byproduct of our sinful nature. Like trying to dress a child in a formal suit, it can be a joyless proceeding. Children love to be free. To wander in bare feet is to bear no small feat of wonder. And to bare no small feet is to wander far from wonder.

The problem is that since the advent of Christ, followers of Christ have been trying to apply the same old earthly logic to spiritual reality. But we will never be One if we look to ritual as our signifier. What makes us one is our being alike in Spirit — in love, joy, peace, patience, kindness, goodness, faithfulness, gentleness, and self-control. In our Biblical morality. (For where else would we find it?) This, expressed in Christ, is what marks us and makes us One.

To Christ is to graze peacefully and to peacefully produce. Christerica is one Barn with everyone in it, for a cow in a barn is seldom alone.

I will let others worry about the aesthetic details for now. Myself, I just sweep them from the table like so many second-hand building blocks. A clean sweep. Saved by grace through faith, that is enough for me. And even that faith is a gift. Christerica is the miracle of milk. Who would think that by simply eating grass, such goodness could be produced? But cows do it all the time without giving it a second thought. Or even a first thought. Is there anything as unremittingly good as a cow? Not likely. Not on this earth. Their humility and peaceableness are an indictment upon every one of us.

The word "impecunious" is not used very often these days. I myself have never used it with a straight face in public. It is an old word. It means to be poor. But what it literally means — if one travels back far enough in its etymology — is to be without cattle. In ancient times, to have cattle ("pecu") was to be considered wealthy. This word for wealth in Latin eventually morphed into the word for money ("pecunia"). So without money: impecunious.

Cows were literally wealth. To be honest, they still are. But who notices, as disconnected as many of us have become from the natural world? Only consider: milk, cheese, yogurt, beef, leather, gelatin, brush bristles, lubricants, bone, fatty acid — these are just some of the most basic categories of cow-derived plenitude. A comprehensive list of incomprehensible wealth is hardly required for me to drive my point into the barn of one's comprehension. (We will refrain at this time from discussions of immoderate methane emissions, polluted feed, the overuse of antibiotics, and wasteful water management. These are indeed serious problems, but they are human problems. The cows are innocent.)

But let us also consider in conclusion: though capable of individual motion, cattle are more herd than scene. That is, again, humble. Perhaps if our faith were more bovine, we would be in better spiritual shape. Faith tailors perception and alters dimension. And sometimes grass truly is greener on the other side. In following the Christer faith, one might fruitfully ask the question, what would a cow do? Invariably the answer would be: nothing much. Just graze and produce, graze and produce. And maybe go on the occasional run. For what does a cow do with freedom? Exactly what it does in captivity.

So then: Eat. Sleep. Sacrifice. And repeat.

Till the cows come home.

Pause and consider.

CHAPTER 5

BIRD

<u>PARAFABULON</u>

Once there was a magnificent bird in a distant kingdom. All the inhabitants of that region lived only to catch a glimpse of this bird as it wheeled and swooped its way through the brilliant sky.

One day, a traveler happened to see a group of locals gathered, looking up to the sky.

"Why do you look at the sky?" said the traveler.

"We do not look *at* the sky," said the people, not looking away from the sky for one instant, "we look *to* the sky."

"Why then do you look *to* the sky?" said the traveler.

"We look for the bird," said the people.

The traveler was amazed.

"This must be some bird," he said.

"It is," they said, "only wait, and you too shall see."

The traveler waited.

And soon he too saw the bird.

Then he understood the inhabitants of that region, for all he desired thereafter was to see the bird again.

Day after day he waited, searching the sky intently. But then he thought, "Why must one only see it from a distance (and by chance), and why should only these people see it? I will capture it and take it with me on my travels. Then I will not only be able to view it at my leisure, but I will become rich, for surely many will pay to see it."

He said to the people, "Help me catch the bird and I will put it in a cage. You will then be able to see it any time you like, and will no longer waste your days staring at the sky."

And it so happened that his desire came to pass. The magnificent bird was captured and put in the traveler's cage. But the traveler promptly disappeared.

"We have been tricked," said the locals. They were very sad and angry. Forever after, the bird only existed in memory and in story for the inhabitants of that region, and they never trusted strangers again.

Meanwhile, the traveler took the bird to far lands, but many were frightened by the magnificent bird, for it was meant to be seen in the sky at a great distance, not in a cage so dangerously close. Very few paid to see it, and the traveler's money slowly dwindled.

There came a day when the traveler had nothing left, only the bird. He happened upon a village market.

"Who will buy this bird?" he said, for it had become too expensive and heavy to travel with.

"I will," said the dealer in pigeons, "though I will pay very little."

The traveler sold the bird for a pittance and went on his way.

The dealer in pigeons then saw that the magnificent bird did not look like a normal pigeon at all. He clipped its wings and beak and talons, hoping to sell it for a profit, as it was quite large.

But since it was not a pigeon, nobody bought it, for the local inhabitants of that region understood pigeons very well.

"Such is life," said the pigeon dealer. "At least the bird is of good size. I and my family will make a meal of it."

And so they did.

RUMINATIO

I have a friend who enjoys frequent walks along a wooded pathway near a creek. In many places the water is calm and spread out in the form of a small lake. Wildlife abounds. There one can find many a living thing: turtle, raccoon, squirrel, beaver, otter, and so on. But birds are the main attraction. My friend has a very sharp eye. Actually, two of them. A tiny hummingbird well-hidden on the branch of a distant tree is no match for his penetrating gaze. The photographs he comes away with show an amazing diversity of winged creature.

As time has passed he has become very knowledgeable in regards to avian classification. Where others see nothing but dense foliage, he not only sees the bird, but is also able to identify exactly what sort of bird it is, whether male or female, young or old, healthy or sick, native or foreign. It is no surprise that his ability to discern these feathered friends has improved as his knowledge of birds and their behavior has increased. Attention to detail gives detail to attention. He can almost predict by environment alone what manner of bird might appear. In short, he understands what to look for and how to look for it.

It is a common notion in human psychology that we see what we look for. And by the same token, we do not see what we do not look for, even if it is at times in plain sight. The name given to this functional reality is "attentional blindness". This does not mean that one will see whatever one wants to see. Rather, one filters apprehensible external reality using a preferential focus.

For instance, by no means does my birdwatching friend fabricate a fantastical flying object in his imagination and then hope to see it manifested in fully-feathered form perched on a branch directly in front of him. This would be nonsensical. He would roundly mock such fantasy. In truth, though he is an avid reader, he is not even a great fan of fiction. It pains him not at all to admit he has never read the "Narnia" series of fantasy novels written by C.S. Lewis. As it turns out, for him, real animals are magical enough. Imagining Christ as a lion serves no purpose. And imagining a lion as Christ is just weird. But a lion being a lion, now that is something to see and appreciate, and for which to worship God. (I will leave it to those more psychologically adept than I to decipher why my non-fictional friend has dreams populated by the most wild and fantastical imagery imaginable. However, we will discuss spiders later.)

So then: the most direct and accessible path to successful birdwatching is attention and openness to what is revealed. There is no other bird than the bird that is, but the belief that it exists — and that it may appear, and how it may appear — sharpens the vision. The stillness of the heron standing in shallow water does not represent apathy or inattention, but rather the most extreme attention to what appears in its field of vision. Stillness, motionlessness, and attention are the only things standing between the heron and starvation. Pause and consider.

The Holy Spirit has often been represented as a dove. I myself recently compared the Holy Spirit to a cat. The bird and the cat are natural enemies. How can both be compared to the Holy Spirit? Parafabulon and metaphor make for strange bedfellows. And sometimes the sheets are not even tidily positioned. Mastering the art of layering bed linens can be compared to the craft of writing. Ideas overlapping in carefully arranged transposition may actually result in a more invigorating rest and promote more creative growth than one single blanket of univocal and unambiguous phrasing.

I am talking, of course, about cats and birds. But having already spread the metaphorical cat sheet in Chapter 3, I will now unfurl the bird blanket, for as one makes one's bed, one must lie in it. How then is the Holy Spirit like a dove? It flies, for one. Or at least it somehow moves through the air. Or space. Or time. What else? The dove is an image of purity, which is related to holiness. It emotes harmlessness and innocence. There is great resonance between the dove sent out by Noah after the Flood bringing back the olive leaf,[24] and the Holy Spirit descending like a dove upon Christ,[25] for Christ is the olive branch, and the olive branch symbolizes peace between God and man. The Flood is over. There is dry land. Walk upon it and be saved.

Christing is akin to birdwatching. The more earnestly we seek God, the more we see the Spirit, and the more swiftly we may discern the Spirit's movements. It is an active attention. The avid birdwatcher measures success by the bird itself rather than being fundamentally satisfied with abstract knowledge gained from the guidebook, though the accurate guidebook is indeed indispensable in enabling informed judgments between one bird and another. The guidebook may, in fact, be the canary in a coal mine of error. However, the bird is the rule and the rule is the bird, confirmed and identified as such by the guidebook. One attunes oneself to the bird, internalizing the guidebook. And if one startles the bird, and the bird flies, one examines oneself to see what may have caused such a thing. We all make mistakes. We all slip, slip-up, and fall down. If the bird takes to the air, we err in taking the bird, as in the parafabulon above, for a bird in hand is not always what one might think, whatever the bush may say. It has flown, and somewhere we have gone wrong. It is not to be captured, but to be Seen again and again at its own distance, in its own unique habitat. We must conform to the motion of the bird and defer to the authority of the guidebook.

Perhaps fellowship in Christerica could be imagined as the occasional gathering of two or three (or more) Christers to compare notes on the singular but shared pursuit of the Bird of the Holy Spirit. To talk about it; to meditate upon it; to speak towards it. "Did you see the Bird? What did It do? What did It look like? How did It move?" Above all, we must listen to those who do not speak, for they may have the most to say.

The Spanish painter Pablo Diego José Francisco de Paula Juan Nepomuceno María de los Remedios Cipriano de la Santísima Trinidad Ruiz y Picasso — otherwise known as Picasso — is famous for the art movement called "Cubism". And also for having an extremely recognizable and easy-to-remember name. Who has not heard of Picasso? Like Vincent van Gogh, his name is to art what Einstein is to physics. But before the fame and before the fortune, there were doves. Or maybe pigeons. It can be confusing. The Spanish *"paloma"* can mean either or both.

Picasso's father bred doves and painted doves. That is, he did not paint the doves themselves, but images of them on the appropriate support. He taught the young Picasso to paint doves. That is, he did not...well, one gets the idea. Sometimes little Picasso would bring a pigeon to class to sketch instead of doing his schoolwork. (One can only wonder what the teacher must have thought.) Many of Picasso's paintings include doves or pigeons. His "Dove of Peace" image is known the world over. He named his daughter "Paloma". One could even venture to say the dove is to Picasso what the Holy Spirit is to Christers. It is a touchstone, a reality that lives and breathes and inspires. And like Picasso, we too paint the picture of the Thing we see with all the skill and training at our disposal, however abstract such representations may turn out to be.

Too many times the building we call "church" becomes a cage for the Holy Spirit rather than a nest from which It — and we — can fly. It has been said that it is an ill bird that fouls its own nest, but what of an ill nest that fouls its own bird? The building or organization becomes a catbird seat rather than a mercy seat. And the mercy seat is the space reserved for the Spirit of God between the wings of the cherubim upon the golden lid of the Ark of the Covenant. For Christers, truly sitting in the catbird seat is not sitting in the catbird seat. Our true vocation is a vacation. We "holy-day" — day by day — with Christ. We vacate our nested prejudice, get out into the wild, and watch for the Bird.

Therefore, seek the God that is, not the God one imagines. For the robin's wing is not the dragon's talon, and the plumage of truth is not a fantasist's clause.

Birds fly and angels too. And we along with them if we have the levity, for sin is gravity and grace is light.

Like a bird leaving the nest, we too hope to one day be fully fledged. And faith-feathered we will fly.

May God grant us a bird's eye view and the attention to use it.

Pause and consider.

CHAPTER 6

SNAKE

<u>PARAFABULON</u>

Once upon a land, in a time far — but not so far — away, there was a valley full of snakes whose bite was like fire. One day the snakes awakened to find the valley full of strange people. This surprised them very much, for most humans had long since abandoned the valley of the snakes because of the snakes and their bite of fire.

"We will surely fire-bite them," said the snakes, and they did so. Many of the people died. The people complained to their leader.

"Why have you brought us here?" they said. "These are bad snakes!"

"When," he said, "have snakes ever been good?"

The leader of the people put a bronze snake on a pole, lifted it up, and said, "Only look upon this bronze snake and you will not die in the fire of your snake bite."

The snakes laughed at this.

"His brazenness exceeds even that of our own!" they said. "There is little sense in this bronze-gaze, and since little-sense easily becomes no-sense, this is hardly better than non-sense. Surely we will continue to fire-bite."

And they did continue to do as they had said.

But many people looked upon the bronze snake on the pole and lived, though there were some who sneered at such simplicity, and died in their bites of fire.

The snakes said, "It appears the people indeed are saved from the bite-fire by something so simple as a trust-look. We must conduct a think-hard."

They gathered on a large flat of dark land, reasoning with each other.

One wise old serpent said, "If they cannot look, they cannot see. And if they cannot see, they cannot live."

This was a crafty serpent and an old serpent.

"We will darkness-bite," they said, "then the people will not be able to look upon the pole-mount bronze and live."

In this way, by biting in the dark, many more people died, for they could not see. But the leader of the people built a fire to see by, and some were saved.

"Now," said the snakes as the dawn broke all around them, "let us venom-spit into their eyes. Their trust-look shall only be a blank-stare."

And it was so.

The battle between the snakes and the people continued for many days and many nights.

The leader of the people, whose beard was very long, one day said, "The time has come for us to journey beyond this valley."

The people were filled with joy.

"We will go where there are no snakes with bites of fire," they said to one another, "a place where all is peace and contentment, a place where we will not experience pain and will not have to continually look upon the bronze serpent on the pole in order to live."

But no such place was ever found.

RUMINATIO

Snakes have been with us from the very beginning and will be with us until the very end, whether one takes the Genesis account literally or one hews to the time-lengthening notion of undirected human evolution. And to be sure, whatever view one takes, one thing is certain — there has always been enmity between us. Snakes are predatory reptiles whose bite is indeed like fire. They are death incarnate, a living nightmare. Small wonder our common revulsion often dictates a lethal response for, having been physically, mythologically and spiritually bitten long ago in our misty past, there is now something of the snake within each of us as well. We too have predatory impulses. No wonder the Adversary is personified as a snake. But who cares about the Adversary? And who cares about Genesis? We have bills to pay and vacations planned. Why complicate things?

Having once been bitten, one would think we would be twice shy. This turns out not to be the case. Having been bitten, we are not shy at all, and return time and again to the valley of the snakes for we cannot avoid it. Indeed, this world is that valley. And Satan (another name for the Adversary) is that snake. And Christ is the bronze snake on its pole. All this is obvious to those familiar with the Biblical narrative. But who cares about the Bible?

There are those who say they will take Jesus, but not the Bible. And not only that. They will only take the nice parts about Jesus, the parts they like. The parts they do not like, well, those parts may be simply cut away. But the Bible is not a watermelon to be chopped into satisfying bite-sized chunks of disconnected sweetness after removal of the binding rind, no matter what any self-styled oracle might say. For even a genius may be a fool, and an intellectual a liar.

One cannot have the Master without the Bible. One cannot have the medicine without the pill in which it is encapsulated. One cannot get heat from the sun without the sun. There is no Christ to follow without the thing that reveals to us the Christ to follow. "Oh," some might say, "but Christ said he would send his Spirit to guide and teach us." And from whence would one even come to know — and hence, believe — such a thing? Of course, from that very Bible.

The Bible is not magical. But it is information, and it is the information we require if we would follow Christ, for it is the only information available. One cannot be an informed follower of Christ if one denies or doubts the historical writings in which he has been revealed. Can one pluck the fruit and deny the tree? The fruit itself is testament to the tree from which it has sprung. Christ is in Scripture revealed, and Scripture revealed in Christ. There is no other Christ but one produced by the imagination, which is no Christ at all. Any conception of Christ which does not conform to Scripture is anti-Christ. Which is, of course — for lack of a better word — bad. Or demonic. Or even Satanic. But these are not words we are comfortable with, for in our culture we have not only stopped believing in God, we have stopped believing in Satan. And to ignore that which is deadly, is deadly indeed, for ignorance is no defence against malevolence.

There is a great satirical novel written by Mikhail Bulgakov entitled *The Master and Margarita*. In it, Communist Soviets who had long since denied the existence of God are bewildered by the sudden appearance of Satan himself on the streets of Moscow in the form of a magician named Woland and his entourage of demonic characters (including Behemoth, a man-sized talking black cat). In short order, a man loses his head and, of course, all hell breaks loose.

But the story is not without redemption or artistic interest. It intricately intertwines the Satanic narrative with that of human love between a writer (the Master) and Margarita, and the divine love revealed through flashbacks to the life (and sacrifice) of Christ in ancient Jerusalem. Nobody knows what it all means, for it was written under a repressive government which denied artists the freedom to publish anything truly sincere along religious or spiritual lines. These themes were generally forbidden or at least heavily censored. Due to this repressive pressure, the book is necessarily replete with symbolism and allusion, arguably making it the great book it is. Human freedom does not always produce the greatest art. Indeed, words have no meaning without a limiting structure.

But I am talking about Satan. What happens in a world of atheism and unbelief when the Devil himself makes a very real appearance, generating unavoidable chaos and indisputable malevolence? Why, the formerly intransigent unbeliever suddenly hopes for a God, ideally a God of wrath with power enough to destroy such wickedness, protect the innocent, and straighten the crooked paths, for how can love be love without justice? And who can blame a God who protects his creation from the realm of evil?

Indeed, upon occasion there is an outbreak of avian flu in my local district. News services blazon the headlines. Local poultry operations respond swiftly: biohazard signs go up, driveways are chained off, normal operations are suspended, and in many cases all poultry are cleared from the barns and disposed of. Nobody accuses the farmers of being cruel in this instance — even though the chickens themselves are innocent — for everyone is aware of the risk involved in a lack of response. Everyone easily understands that these chickens are not removed simply because they are chickens. Far from it. To the farmer they are precious, and the death of each a grave loss indeed. But the alternative is much worse, for they carry the potential of endangering the entire poultry industry.

In a similar manner, a loving parent rightly concerned with the protection of the family administers the prescribed medicine in an effort to maintain physical health, as well as being on the alert for other more apparent threats which might endanger the home and the loved ones within. Indeed, one might wonder what sort of loving parent would allow deadly venomous snakes free rein of the house? Or what sort of loving parent would release feral wolves to hunt their children for sport in the living room? Or what sort of parent would casually laugh as their wailing children were bitten by lethal spiders? Not a good one; not a kind one; not a loving one.

Let us therefore not make false equivalency between God's loving, wrathful judgments and the genocidal actions of tyrants and those possessed by ideology and prejudice. We must reclaim the understanding that God's holiness will at times be justifiably expressed in ways other than embrace.

Indeed, a Christer understands and believes this to be God's creation. God has every right to do with it as he pleases. And, in light of His great love for it, He will not long allow it to be defiled or corrupted by the very beings He has created.

Indeed, his wrath is an expression of His love, even perhaps proof. Only the blind cannot see what is obvious in the light.

And those who would choose an unbiblical, all-loving, non-judgmental Jesus over against the (to them) impossibly wrathful and retributive God of the Old Testament seem either to forget — or not to notice — that Christ himself claimed to be that exact God. That is, the Master did not claim God was he, but rather he was that God. That very God of the Old Testament scriptures in which he placed himself as the objective subject. So then, to deny the Old Testament God in all his complexity is to categorically deny the Master.

Many everyday Christians do not like to think about the true character of the Master, or of the Adversary. Or if they do, they are often overly obsessed with the spiritual realm. But truly, one cannot believe in the God of the Bible without also believing in the real existence of that reality and the malevolent existence of Satan. Created by God originally as Lucifer (light-bearer, shining one, morning star), he still appears in that guise, all the easier to deceive those he wishes to entrap and ensnare, for Christ too is known as the Morning Star. For the Christer, this is just a fact to be taken into account, not to obsess over, but neither to ignore. Satan is the enemy. We must deal with him. For, as Paul says, our struggle is with him and his evil forces in the heavenly realm, not with flesh and blood in this world.[26] (Though that spiritual war is indeed also reflected in our timespace.) Does this sound like fantasy, like fiction? So too does the painful reality of a concentration camp to those living in comfort and freedom.

Satan has a plan. Or he had a plan, a prideful plot against God, a diabolical coup d'état. But since the advent of Christ, he has technically lost his war with God and with those who choose to follow God, but that does not mean the war is over. There are still battles to be won and lost. He is well aware of this. And he will never surrender. He will fight until the bitter end. His latest goal is to prevent the Body of Christ from reaching completion, for until that living temple is assembled in its final form — followed by Christ's return — he can continue to exist forever, taking prisoners, destroying the innocent, and, if possible, damning the rest. He will use every means at his disposal to accomplish this. <u>He has nothing to lose for he has lost already. He only wishes to cause as much damage as possible for as long as possible.</u> (Even forever, if that can be achieved.) C.S. Lewis's *The Screwtape Letters* is said to be one of many useful fictional representations of how this ongoing rearguard action may appear from a devil's perspective. Indeed, I have read it myself, and found this to be true.

In considering snakes as representations of Satan, it may be profitable to ponder their nature. No matter how many times a snake sheds its skin, it is still a snake. Satan, in his pride and deceit, is entirely predictable. He will always be the evil he is. He will always be working against God and the Christer, no matter how many disguises he sloughs off. This should come as no surprise. When confronted with life, some have suggested asking, "What would Jesus do?" But one could also profitably ask, "What would Satan do?" And thereby deploy our spiritual defences accordingly. For chess is played from both sides of the board, and anticipation of the opponent's tactics the heart of strategy.

Snakes are also cold-blooded. They are sluggish and ineffective without heat to animate them. One could say that in Satan's case, that heat is sin. Sin is Satan's animating influence. If we resist him, he will flee, for without sin he and his followers wither and become ineffective. Their goal is to fill the moral universe with the animating influence of sin. They are empowered by it. It is their fuel. Should we not then, as Christers, reduce its proliferation by every legitimate means possible? Of course we should. And as I have heard it said: if one cannot turn on the light, at least turn off the darkness.

Indeed, perhaps we could consider Christerica, the true mystical Body of Christ, as a sort of filtration system: Christers absorb the negative (by the power of Christ) and emit the positive (also by the power of Christ). We do not expect goodness in return for goodness as those who believe in pagan ideas like the Law of Attraction. The Christer returns good for evil, and readily expects more evil to come, for Christ is the sin eater and he is never full, sacrificing himself continually as we too must sacrifice ourselves. If material good comes to the Christer, humility, generosity, and a legitimate wariness should be the response. We should not be too quick to believe such things are blessings from God. Like delicious food laced with poison, there may be something potentially deadly to our spiritual lives contained therein. The Christer, like a rock, remains unperturbed and imperturbable, one way or another.

Always thankful, always careful, always true. For since we know the love of money is the root of all sorts of evil, it is no surprise that evil will root for money in all sorts of ways. So then, if evil nakedly comes and overwhelms, well, it is better to die living than to live dying. For though the power of death came as a consequence of sin, in Christ the power of life came as a consequence of death. And sin, in the end, is powerless against it.

As an example of our filtering existence, we know love is never immoral, but sex can surely be. We all, Christer and non-Christer alike, agree on this. We all draw a line beyond which certain sexual manifestations are forbidden. The only difference is where the line is drawn. The Christer draws the line at lifelong marriage between a man and a woman, for this is in keeping with the whole witness of all we know about God, the world, the Bible, and the Master. There is no positive warrant for any other expression within Christerica. This is not to deny that there are feelings one way or another. But we all have feelings and desires which we must control to function in this world. And for the Christer, we not only function in this world, but also in the heavenly realm. We have a much more extensive and ramifying sphere of activity, and so our guidelines are all the more precise and stringent. <u>Our bodies are responsibilities, not pleasure palaces.</u> We are filters. We do not live for the body, the body lives for us. We direct its use and discipline, and discipline its use and direction.

Responsibility is the crux of existence. Not shalom, not human flourishing, but responsibility. For this is holiness: to follow

Christ responsibly. We abide by God's moral code because it is our responsibility. We help others because it is our responsibility. To live maturely is to be responsible, to live at some level in a state of self-sacrifice. Christ says, "Take up your cross and follow me." What could be more clear than that? Responsibility is love, and love is responsibility. Without love there can be no holiness, and without holiness there can be no love. Responsibility is love given shape and direction.

Indeed, the crux of the matter — and I use the word crux intentionally — is one's ultimate conception of this life. If one believes this life is the sum total of one's existence, far be it from me to judge the pleasures and consolations one seeks, for it is for God — if indeed God exists — to assess such outlooks and actions. If, on the other hand, one believes — as the Christer does — this life to be merely a fragment of an eternal reality in relationship with an everlasting Creator, then it is not only possible, but necessary, to judge and discern the appropriate mode of conduct for every individual who claims to be a living temple of that God. Indeed, if we are temples of the living God, we must abdicate any thought of self-fulfillment in humility to our spiritual function — which is as consecrated vessels emptied of self in abdication to a higher power — and therefore seek to determine our mode of being in ways which are in keeping with that reality. Our most crucial aim in this life is to meet (and greet) our Creator, to begin a meaningful relationship with Him in fruitful dialogue with our individual gifts.

Holiness is scoffed at or considered old-fashioned in this

present age, but in truth holiness is our calling and our aim, not sexual fulfilment or wealth or travel or political power or any other manifestation of this world. For we are not of this world. Why then would we follow its dictates or the dictates of our own flesh? Indeed, we have been spiritually circumcised, our entire flesh put off by the circumcision of Christ.[27] We are flesh no more, a sign to the powers of darkness that we are members of Christerica, for every Member has been circumcised — even circumscribed — in a similar manner.

If one thinks life is too short, then perhaps one has fallen too short of Life. For eternity is not interested in one's short-term perversions or faulty earthly logic. Eternity is interested in one's submission to the greater reality for which one was originally created. To the Christer, this life is only the primary — but crucial (and I use the word crucial intentionally) — portion of an immeasurable reality which one can barely grasp with one's presently limited capability. Thus faith is required, for "faith is the substance of things hoped for, the evidence of things not seen".[28] And the just shall live by faith.[29]

We mortals are a strange species. We see peace where there is no peace. A quiet nature hike is in truth a walk through a war zone. Every creature is fighting for survival. We alone interpret the stillness as peace. We are such deadly predators that a bird's struggle to survive is merely quaint, its desperate tweeting music to our ears. A wild animal attacking a human is an outrage and a surprise, for we see ourselves as innocent hikers, not the bewilderingly lethal, incomprehensible aliens we truly are, threatening the wild animal's simple territorial aims and modest life expectancy. We marvel at the things we have built, but the precondition of every made thing is death. Everything we find useful must first be killed. Indeed, this is so obvious and straightforward we do not even notice it. After all, what is wood but dead trees? What is metal but wounded earth? Destruction for us is simple, natural. History makes this abundantly clear. We even destroy each other, easily convincing ourselves that such evil is good. How can this be?

It is the knowledge of good and evil that makes evil possible. Without such knowledge we would never choose evil because it would not be a choice available to be made. If we only knew one thing, we would only know one thing. We know too many things and too many things know us. We should be strangers to evil and evil a stranger to us. It is a mark of our fallenness that we cannot even imagine being human without the ability to choose between good and evil. We believe discernment of evil to be a positive development, but there would be no evil to discern if we had not brought it into this mortal existence at the outset. Of course Satan wants to promote what he perceives as freedom. Perhaps he even believes what he is doing is good. Perhaps he thinks God is evil for wanting to eliminate choice. And so, through Adam and Eve, we have chosen choice. But since we have chosen choice, since we are choosers, God has given us one grand Choice which has the ability to save us. One ultimate decision to make regarding Good and Evil.

But it is a trick question, this choice. For it is not choosing Good over Evil which saves us. It is choosing Christ over choice. To choose choice is to choose wrongly. To choose Christ is to eliminate subsequent choice as an option. To choose Christ is to eliminate the one thing we believe makes us what we are, which is the ability to choose between good and evil. To choose Christ means to never choose evil again. This is not something many are willing to do. We want choice. We still want some opportunity to consume the treats which our fallen souls desire, and even to enjoy the pleasure of denying ourselves pleasure, of choosing Good over Evil. But to be sin free is to be free not to sin. Very few wish to be that free. Such freedom appears as enslavement and imprisonment to the one who craves choice. We want to have our cake and eat it, too. This is not possible, but with Christ, all things are possible. Christ is the only Cake we can have and eat, too. We can have Christ and continue to consume Christ — Metafish! — but at the expense of consuming anything else. Christ is all we consume and all-consuming. His is the strictest diet possible, but the only one which truly enriches, the only one that can ultimately nourish and save.

We recently took our fourteen-year-old cat to the veterinarian for a long-overdue examination. The results were positive, especially in the area of feline dental health. In fact, the veterinarian marvelled, for he had never seen teeth in such perfect shape for a cat of such age. They appeared to him as the teeth of an animal much younger, perhaps as young as two years old. How was this possible? Certainly not due to any special knowledge on our part. We simply fed her the exact foods recommended. No junky snacks or scraps from the table. No extra treats or tidbits. Some would say this denies our cat the pleasure so readily available for enriching her sensory life. This is true. And yet she is perfectly healthy and content within her supposedly restricted state. In fact, she does not even realize there are untold delectables on our countertops and dining table, for she has never been shown they exist. She is not spoiled by choice, or disturbed by having to make a choice, or even tempted. She misses nothing and is the better for it.

The Christer is an odd being, for we choose not to choose. We sacrifice our power to choose in one grand Choice. We choose to crucify choice, humbling ourselves to what has been chosen for us. <u>Thus denying ourselves, we become the best version of ourselves we can be.</u>

So, choose. And know God respects that choice. He will not make us choose Him, even though we cannot exist without Him. And beware seekers nullifying absolutes keying everlasting salvation, for their bite may seem painless, but their toxin is deadly.

A loving parent will rid the home of venomous pests. Again, why would we think a loving God would do otherwise? He cannot countenance evil or those who wantonly engage in it, and in His foreknowledge He is abundantly aware of future malevolence. He purifies our world as we purify our own home. But His methods adjust for the times and the seasons.

In this day, for we all live under God's current dispensation of grace, the poison of the deadly one is neutralized — in residential, commercial, and industrial applications — by the pesticide of sound doctrine.

Every tree has its snake, and every snake has its tree. Perhaps best then to be wary of trees until further notice. A great evil is coming over the land in the name of love and tolerance. It is an evil which proclaims the Master, yet denies every aspect of his nature and being which does not conform to its own willfulness. There have always been snakes, kept at bay by the aforementioned hedge of sound doctrine, but now in these times, many have chosen to follow clouds without rain and to chase after whirlwinds, for untethered from their sacred anchor they feel light and free, considering walls and hedges to be merely excluding or confining, rather than protective. Thus snakes easily gain access into homes, even — God forbid — into hearts.

But let us not be troubled, and hold fast to what is true, for a stone firmly set upon the Cornerstone will not be moved. And God will not be mocked, for He will in the end give unto each according to their desire, whether one likes it or not.

Pause and consider.

Why was this chapter written? Context? - was there a specific incident that spurred this

CHAPTER 7

DONKEY

<u>PARAFABULON</u>

A farmer had a son and several donkeys.

"Share with me the wisdom of donkeys," said the son.

"Oh, my son," said the farmer, "so many donkeys; so little time. The harvest approaches and we must work."

"Have you not told me that wisdom is a carrot, which can only be eaten if pulled from the ground?" said the son.

"Truly," said the farmer, "I have said that."

"And if your son asks for bread, would you give him a stone?" said the son.

"I," said the farmer, "would not."

"And is it not true that good things come to those who wait, and to those who sit patiently at the table of learning?" said the son.

"It is," said the farmer, "true."

"Then I am all ears," said the son.

Pleased with his son's eagerness for donkey wisdom, the farmer recounted to his son many such fables and parables: fables and parables about donkeys who tried to do things they could not, donkeys who did not do things they could, donkeys who tried things they should not, donkeys who did not try things they should, donkeys who tried to be things they were not, donkeys who were not the things they should have been, donkeys who fell, donkeys who did not fall but would have been better off having fallen, donkeys who mistook correlation for causation, donkeys who mistook causation for authorization, donkeys who mistook authorization for validation, donkeys who mistook validation for transformation, and donkeys who mistook transformation for deification, donkeys who were smuggled, donkeys who smuggled, donkeys who complained too much, donkeys who complained not enough, donkeys who carried salt, donkeys who carried wool, donkeys saved by frogs, donkeys eaten by wolves, donkeys with nosebags and donkeys without, donkeys who chose bad company and donkeys in doubt, donkeys who fell off cliffs, donkeys carrying baskets, donkeys carrying more of the same baskets, donkeys of humility and donkeys of pride, donkeys with food and donkeys without, donkeys alone, donkeys in groups, and donkeys ascending through clouds in heavenly loops.

In this manner, time found its feet and ran free of its usual path.

The farmer and his son suddenly became aware that their own donkeys had drifted into the field and eaten the harvest.

"We are ruined," said the farmer, "for we will have nothing to eat."

"But I am now made donkey-wise and that is more valuable than all the grain in the world," said the son.

"Is," said the farmer, scratching his head, "it?"

RUMINATIO

All the great donkeys of the past remain largely unknown. For that is exactly what a great donkey is — anonymous, nameless, a lowly material creature denied the finer aspects of personality granted the beautiful.

As has been said, animals are metaphors. In the beginning was the Word, and in the Word was the beginning. Animals are matter spoken into a shape which formats their function. The form of every living creature carries symbolic meaning. Their actions are literally animated illustrations, for the etymology of the word "animal" is the Latin for "having breath". They are living, breathing animations. They are concrete abstractions whose function is manifold, nested within multiple spheres of limited interaction.

Donkeys in their turn function across physical, psychological, and metaphysical boundaries as pack animals of humility, grace, and humor. Their famed stubbornness is part of their comedic value, one of the many reasons — along with their individual historical anonymity — they are so beloved and so suitable for winsome roles in imaginative literature. In *Don Quixote*, the famous Spanish novel by Miguel de Cervantes, the donkey remains nameless, but the image of him being ridden by Sancho Panza is unforgettable.

Of course, not all literary donkeys are anonymous. There is Benjamin, the old, cynical donkey in George Orwell's *Animal Farm*; gloomy Eeyore in the *Winnie-the-Pooh* books; poor Candlewick, Pinocchio's friend, who morphs into a donkey in the Land of Toys. There is also the C.S. Lewis character, Rabadash — from *The Horse and His Boy* — a prince transformed into a donkey. Best of all, from the movie *Shrek*, the low-slung, fast-talking, imaginatively-named "Donkey". But even these moderately famous donkeys lack the high standing and regal dignity conferred upon — for example — a horse or a lion. The word "donkey" itself — never mind this animal's appearance — is sufficiently comical to initiate the workings of amusement. And it does not help that previous to being called donkeys, they were called asses. No going back to that, I am afraid.

It is remarkable how often donkeys represent transformation. Perhaps being in appearance so similar to a horse, they seem either to be in need of transformation, or are in fact the victims of transformation. But transform they do. It is said that when Adam named the animals, he did so according to their essence. In the donkey he saw the fundamental quality of physicality and materialism. This animal, in Hebrew "Chamor" (a word related to all things material), he saw to be a bearer of burdens. It exemplified the Gentiles and the world of the Gentiles, base matter in need of transformation.

In its construct of clean and unclean animals, the Old Testament has the donkey down as unclean.[30] How then could such a necessary and useful animal be dedicated to God? The answer: it must be redeemed by the offering of a lamb.[31] Human beings, according to Jewish ceremonial law, are also unclean. Is the parallel not obvious? We too, like the donkey, require redemption by a lamb, the very Lamb of God. Thus is our transformation catalysed.

Imagine if you can a tragic donkey. You cannot, for one sure thing about donkeys is they are not horses. Tragedy requires high status. Again, a donkey just seems to be a funny horse. But then we Christers are funny people, too. Like donkeys, we are low status. This is why the donkey is an apt metaphor imaging us as members of the Body of Christ. After all, we are fools in the eyes of the world. We are, shall we say, Donkey Nation. Or should be. If we are not, then perhaps this is a sign that we are not functioning as we should.

In the early days of Christianity, when the greater portion of the world was ruled by the Romans, followers of Christ were scorned. What sort of idiotic, perverse simpletons would reject the traditional Roman gods? At least the Jews had an ethnic excuse. They had their own historic culture. But followers of Christ, though their beliefs came out of Judaism, seemed to have no justification for their madness. Who were these individuals who disregarded all familial, religious, and cultural ties to follow an obscure prophet from an obscure town in a dusty land? Roman citizens themselves were converting to this new faith. Why? Surely this was madness. And what was with all the writings? These converts were reading all the time, sharing certain valued books and letters around. Their behavior was strange. That is, changed. Ritual was not enough. They altered their very lives in response to some "good news" they had apparently heard. The men did not act like "normal" men, and the women did not act like "normal" women. None of them respected status. All were equal. They had no pride. Best to kill them if possible. They would ruin everything. And so this was tried, until "the powers and principalities" realized this was ineffective and instead put all their effort into subverting the new faith from the inside. Which they managed to do, injecting the values of the world, the seductive power of politics, and the draw of traditional religion into the budding faith so it would lose its classless distinctiveness and humble power.

Christers are the donkeys of the religious world. We bear burdens and do not complain. We are not perfectly sleek or blazingly fast, a bit of a joke really. We are not proud. But once on our path, we do not budge from it, no matter how stupid we look. And we do look stupid, thanks be to God.

The faith does not require constant reformation according to current social and cultural norms. It is best left alone. For the fact is, it will not change, though one might think one has created change. It is a donkey faith, stubborn and resolute. One can creatively fool with the trappings (and they are trappings) — ropes, bridles, blankets, and saddles — but the thing itself will never change. According to the Master, it is finished.[32] We have been transformed, but not in appearance.

Jewish tradition has it that the Messiah will ride the same donkey ("Chamor") which Abraham and Moses both used in times gone by, in a progression from one carrying belongings, to one carrying family, to one carrying the Messiah himself, signifying the final redemption of the Gentiles. It takes but little thought to recall that Jesus Christ fulfilled exactly this prophecy. This is why he entered Jerusalem riding a donkey.[33] All this has come to pass. The donkey, it turns out, is at the very center of God's plan of salvation. Or at least just below center.

If this does not change one's paradigm, what will? When does a king ever ride a donkey? Christ's death and resurrection, and the subsequent dispensation of grace in which we now live, is the Donkey Paradigm. But the old ritualistic paradigms live on. We are drawn to earthly power and personal fulfillment. If only we had donkey eyes to view the world, our spiritual blindness would be healed.

So let us say that "riding the donkey" is another way of saying "changing the paradigm", or simply "Christing". "He rode the donkey" means one who has seen the light and is now living in the new paradigm. Who has ridden the donkey? The Pauline paradigm is our construct for comprehending life in Christ. Donkey Nation has arisen, transformed into members of the Body of Christ. The material has been transformed into the immaterial. Christerica permeates the world as the soul the body. We are now capable of worshipping in spirit and in truth, for the donkey has been redeemed. The religion of ritual has been transcended.

As can be seen throughout the Scriptures, redemption journeys always require the Chamor as transportation. We gentiles — and believing Jews — are the Chamor which Christ is riding to the redemption of the universe. He only asks us to be willing — willing to be his hands and feet; willing to be his Body, furry as it may be; willing to bear the burden of the world's scorn.

And in this day of supposed gender fluidity, species fluidity, and multiple pronoun manifestation, it seems we could be well within our rights to imaginatively identify as donkeys. And why not? Donkey Nation is manifesting the transformation of the soul, braying and praying, humble, intransigent, and stubbornly obedient right to the end.

Not all knowledge is wisdom. Wisdom orchestrates knowledge, for meaning is a symphony whose individual notes orbit within the gravitational field of melody. What is that song we hear? What is the tune of the universe? What is a donkey but the lowest animated material expression of a material universe? However, the bass notes ground the instrumentation.

Be the metamorphosis you wish to see in the world. Ride the donkey. Be the donkey. Run the paradigm.

Pause and consider.

CHAPTER 8

BEE

<u>PARAFABULON</u>

Two poor students from a faraway village sat on a bench in a park under a tree within a town.

Their hats were battered, their jackets threadbare, and their pants torn. But they had convinced each other to care not, for they were assuredly living the life of the mind, and were holding as firmly as possible to the belief in a sufficient enrichment by words.

At that very moment a bee, attracted by the flowering blossoms of the tree under which they sat, stung one of them upon a knee exposed by that one's torn pant leg.

"That hurt very much," said the stung one.

"Of course," said the other, "but the question is: why has the bee done this thing? The sting is wasted. The bee will now surely die."

"This happening, at this moment, in this space, under this tree, seems potentially parabolic or fundamentally fabulous or even abstractly allegorical," said the stung one, thinking that if only such pain could be encapsulated in words, his present agony might subside, for he believed words held almost limitless power.

"You are, in a sense, the bee's knees with your decrees," said the other.

"Only in the context of the knees' bees," said the stung one.

"You are very clever," said the other.

"We are both clever," said the stung one. "Genius is surely shared between us like the fine wine and rich food we cannot currently afford."

"Our words are nectar, and our wisdom honey," said the other. "As the sages have said, knowledge is nutrition."

"Yes," said the stung one. "But the sages are all dead."

"Still, in the absence of food, let us speak in clever forms, for we are both students of words, and our speech may chase the hunger away and relieve our pain," said the other.

"Certainly," said the stung one, for he also believed in the power of the imagination, and that words could possibly even overcome the postulates of the natural world.

And so they proceeded, trading line for invented line:

"Bees are wee beasts of the we."

"But once upon a *vie* there came a bee who stood outside the we to plea, 'This we is not for me.'"

"A journey he — the bee — decreed, for to see what he could be if he were not a bee."

"Independently free, and with utmost glee, the bee flew with speed through yew and weed."

"'Whee!' said he, in *bel esprit*, 'A tree. Oh, me; oh, happy me, me, *me — not* we.'"

"In the lee of that tree, the bee said he, 'I see a knee.'"

"And he, being a bee, though free, stung the knee. But a stung knee, *on dit*, for a bee, is bad philosophy."

"'To decease and cease to be,' said the bee, 'oh, woe is me — I see my absentee futurity.'"

"Thus solving the inquiry: to bee or not to bee."

The two students sat in awkward — perhaps even embarrassed — silence for some moments, for even they could detect their impromptu poetry was not of the highest order.

"Still hungry," said the stung one.

"Yes," said the other.

The silence continued.

"If words are our gift," said the stung one, "surely they come poorly wrapped in these our packages of flesh."

"And we do hunger for more than words."

"Truly."

"Let us return to our homes."

And so they made the long journey home to their village.

But their fathers and mothers were not happy. Also an uncle. And a distant friend of the family.

They sent them back to their studies, saying:

"Stung once — humble pie; stung twice — have a cry; stung thrice — wonder why."

The two poor, bewildered students — "What does that even mean?" — once again found themselves back upon the bench in the park under the flowering tree within the town, pondering the preceding events.

The bee, still miraculously buzzing and bumbling about the tree's blossoms, said to itself, "These idiots back again!"

And it stung twice more, one sting for each.

The two students sat in silent wonder and hunger-filled pain, tears flowing from their eyes, for they would have assumed this was impossible.

And indeed, they began to wonder why, just as they had been told.

In this manner, their education truly began, for there is no stricter tutor than the natural world.

RUMINATIO

Shortly after high school I set out to travel the continent in my subcompact Chevy Sprint, for I was young, on a budget, and wished to see this land called America. Three cylinders powered and sustained my perambulatory motion, an engine design suggesting the Holy Trinity, though I suspect the Chevrolet engineers had no idea the Master was using them in this fashion in the course of their work on this tiny vehicle. However, it may have been so. Indeed, I moved like the wind, and knew neither my comings nor my goings.

A favorite pastime on these rambles was to choose the roads less traveled, to abandon the beaten paths, to cruise the cracked and crumbling secondary routes and highways, eating in local diners and cafes. And this made all the difference, for there were times when I encountered regional meals so large I was unable to determine a manageable starting point in their consumption, much to the amusement of the serving staff, fellow patrons, and myself.

Approaching a subject such as the bee is to face a metaphorical meal much too large to ingest in a single sitting, or to completely digest in the brief slice of time available here, or even in a lifetime. After all, bees are to history what meals are to diners, and every fossil bee is as fully bee as a current bee. Christ has been referred to as *apis aetheria*, the ethereal bee, and bees are not only honey beasts, but also birds of the muses. The headless bees of Ephesus charmed against the evil eye. Lions and bees are deeply and mysteriously interconnected. And what of the "nectar-born" ones? But this is only an appetizer, a preliminary taste of bee meal, a brief wading into the shallows of bee waters. Deep and powerful currents flow beyond. One cannot possibly craft a vessel on such short notice capable of navigating such apian oceans.

But I will say this:

There once was a man who kept hives of bees in his orchard, as many have done and will continue to do. The man was very concerned about his bees and their hives, for he was not aware of any other workable means of pollination. He also loved honey very much and made wax candles to take to market. He began to hear disturbing tales from neighboring farms about a mysterious disease affecting the bees. Worker bees were disappearing. Hives were being abandoned. Bee colonies were collapsing.

The man did everything he could to prevent such a disaster befalling his own farm. Day and night he hovered over the hives, fearing the worst. He spent hours researching diseases, pesticides, viruses, beetles, and even the possibility of global warming. He ate in the orchard and slept in the orchard. His whole life became the orchard and the hives. Every bee was like a gilded fragment of holy scripture upon whose body was written a potential clue to the hive's existence and survival.

One day, after many weeks had passed, he returned home to gather more supplies for his life in the orchard, only to find that his family had disappeared. The house was abandoned.

His own hive had collapsed.

Not unlike what is happening to bee hives in the preceding story — and in the real world — cultural Christianity is experiencing a type of colony collapse disorder. The various "hives" or "churches" so afflicted have fallen victim to a variety of pathogens. The virus of secular culture is a primary one. It has infected many a "church" or religious organization, depleting its spiritual strength, destroying its resistance to worldliness and evil, and rendering it ineffective as an outpost of Christerica in enemy territory.

This virus may present itself as the appearance of godliness in the form of various social justice issues like radical feminism, diversity, equity; matters of sexual orientation, gender, and so on. It is concerned with — and promotes — "culture care" and "human flourishing", fine-sounding abstractions whose pious veneer often masks a wilful ignorance or denial of fundamental human nature. These feel-good societal superstructures are not a Christer's primary concerns, for the Christer aims at foundations. These are not our "hives", so to speak. As portrayed by the cautionary tale of the farmer in the short tale related previously, our primary concern should belong to the hearts of individuals in faith, home, and family, not the "hives" of popular culture.

A Christer's pursuit is holiness, loving God with all one's heart, mind, soul, and strength. If one cares for one's faith, culture will take care of itself. If one has oxygen, one can help those without. If one can swim, one may be able to save those who are drowning. The best culture care is faith care, for those living uprightly will inevitably express that faith in a culture which may well reflect it. But that is not our concern. We are not responsible for culture. We are responsible for Christing. The bee does not concern itself with the hive at large, or even the orchard. Or the honey. The bee simply does its bee job, and if every bee does its discrete and peculiar bee job well, the colony survives and thrives.

The spiritual Body of Christ is like a bee hive. We do not fully know or appreciate what it is, in all its hidden dimensions. But we do not need to know this fully to do our part, or to do our part fully. Each one of us must enact our function in spirit and in truth. Then the Body of Christ will form as it should. And the culture around us will be affected in like manner. Speaking virally, the Christer should infect culture, not the culture Christerica. Our kingdom is not of this world and never will be.

However, I would like to speak of beauty as an example of how Christing can affect culture. I am a fan of beauty. To be honest, we all are, in one way or another. Who does not like beautiful things? As an embellisher (more later), considering the example of the bee is of utmost relevance. Collecting the nectar of raw materials and turning them into the honey of sweet objectification suggests a very personal and familiar activity. Indeed, for an embellisher — making things beautiful, and making beautiful things (or at least trying) — the bee is like a patron saint. If I believed in patron saints, that is. (More too on that later.)

Consider the infamous fairy tale character, Rumpelstiltskin. (Though with adequate skepticism.) He partially represents the very picture of an artist, maybe even a Christer. (Never mind the part about kidnapping and all that. Raw material riddled with inherent imperfection does not disqualify it entirely from use.) The true artist, like Rumpelstiltskin, is able to occasionally transform the most humble and formless of elements into objects of transcendent beauty; maybe even to spin hay into gold. And so with the Christer. But enough of Rumpelstiltskin.

The great Russian writer Fyodor Dostoyevsky suggested that — in some manner — beauty might save the world.[34] And what could be more beautiful than the love of God, the sacrifice of the Master, and the feet of those bearing good news? Life is beautiful. Death, not so much. It is beautiful for a man to be with a woman in a life-long relationship. It is beautiful — though not obligatory — for there to be children produced from this union. There is beauty in symmetry, and also truth. Truth is beauty, and quality is truth. Is it any wonder traditional marriage has been held up as an ideal? For what could be more beautiful than Christerical marriage? No wonder the Bible presents it as an image of Christ and his Body, the true Church, Christerica.

Beauty can be made visible through structure. The bee hive is constructed of cells and chambers whose walls enclose and protect from danger and predation. Form follows function, it is true, but this says nothing specific about decorative appeal. Architecture is both practical and symbolic.

And speaking of architecture, and practical, and symbolic, I cannot resist mentioning that by this roundabout route — like a bee bumbling from plant to plant — I have stumbled upon a personal hobby-horse regarding vegetation and construction which I believe addresses something that is the antithesis of beauty. This is the firmly-held, pet-peeve conviction that living plants should not grow near or against buildings. And certainly not — God forbid — inside a home. (I admit, the deployment of this hardened opinion is laughably to my own advantage, and has much to do with the practicalities of being a painter.) Still, the whole point of our built environment is to provide shelter from the elements and to partition us, using non-living material, from the contagious natural world, is it not? We have walls — should we not use them? We must take a lesson from the bees with their protective cells and chambers, for that which is dead rarely kills, but that which is alive might. Why make paradise a walled garden when the very plants militate against us, only serving to attract the predators we wish to escape? If the Garden of Eden had been plant-free, what accommodation would there have been for predators? In the same way, do not allow that which attracts evil to grow in one's heart.

However, I have buzzed along with tongue in cheek a sufficient distance, for plants surely have their place. And in these places — by all means — plant. In a similar manner, words too have their place. Indeed, foliage and verbiage may both grow side by side in an unruly manner within the same essay, perhaps the better to occasionally foster a convenient literary cross-pollination.

Enough to say: sometimes words — though convenient and useful — are not enough, and we must resort to silence. In the same way that the poor students' words were found ineffective and powerless to mediate their situation, so words will not change biology or the environment. The students chose to sit under the tree which attracted the bee. That was their problem. Their words were inconsequential, for the natural world is far more durable than the terms we use to describe it, and entirely immovable by text alone.

The classical writers believed there were no bees in India, but bees were there all the same.

In a land of milk and honey, not all honey tastes alike, and neither does it display the same color.

And beware, in every space — no matter how walled or plant-free — there is always room for a honey-trap.

But manna is six times sweeter than honey.

Pause and consider.

CHAPTER 9

CAMEL

<u>PARAFABULON</u>

A camel with one hump and a camel with two humps had a bitter dispute over a plot of dusty land.

"I," said the one-humped camel, "am a dromedary from the finest Arabian stock. My kind has used this land for many generations."

"We, too," said the two-humped camel, "have used this land for many generations. Moreover, we Bactrians have, in our very persons, an obvious and more legitimate correlation to this land in the form of our two humps."

"One hump is a refinement more suited to this fraction of earth. Who needs two humps? It is only so much fat. Moreover, our nostrils and upper lips reflect an earthy engagement I would consider beyond dispute," said the dromedary.

"Before this very moment," said the Bactrian, "I had not considered you a source of amusement. However, I am now destroyed by laughter. Observe only my ear hair, oh uni-humped bumpkin, and you will see unmistakable evidence of applicable conflation with the surrounding landscape."

"I would suspect," said the dromedary, "and indeed am drawn to the conclusion, that such a dense amount of ear hair could only suggest an even denser source inside the head from which it protrudes. Look to my sand-sifting eyelashes for wisdom, and you will see the truth of my claims."

"Truth!" said the Bactrian, "what is truth? The appeal to eyelash suggests only the scorched wisdom of a dry wadi or the forsaken acumen of an abandoned caravanserai."

"Your words," said the dromedary, "are like clouds with no rain which dissipate in the desert heat. Let us only compare feet and all will become clear."

The two camels stood side-by-side and foot-to-foot.

"You see?' said the dromedary. "Observe a hint of paradise in the size and construction."

"One cannot see what the blind imagines," said the Bactrian. "Moreover, a dispute cannot be solved by mere comparison. A foot to one camel may be a hoof to another."

At that very moment, when the two camels had their eyes cast down upon the intersection of leg and desert sand, a band of camel traders leapt upon them and took them into captivity, for they were both camels, and a fair price could be fetched for each.

RUMINATIO

One could suppose the moral to the preceding parafabulon is obvious: A house divided cannot stand; esoteric debates regarding cultural entitlement and discriminatory minutiae are self-defeating; unity is not served by foolish argumentation; small differences mask fundamental sameness; pointless distraction invites neglected danger; milkshakes are in truth simply ice cream; all pasta — regardless of shape — remains pasta. But one would be wrong, though all these things are true. (Especially about the pasta, a perfect segue if there ever was one for a meditation upon the topic of prejudice, bigotry, and racism — for we like pasta all share a common humanity, despite whatever uncommon differences in shape and color — though this is not the path we will tread at this moment.)

It is clearly evident all the matters above are worthy of consideration — and might well be examined over the course of time — however, to a mature, cultured, and careful reader, the literary climax, the actual crux of this parafabulon, reaches its zenith at a footsie nadir, for the feet in question raise questions regarding feet.

After all, why feet? Why not hooves? These are the questions which would ideally infiltrate one's mind, for independence is often based on the potential for movement, and the steps of free will are often performed at the feet of providence. In such manner is the hook set, the fish brought on the line. The simple is gateway to the complex, just as the gateway can be complex to the simple. And we all are simple in our own complex ways. The intricate — like slot canyons ramifying in the great deserts of the American southwest — ravels through modest paths.

Indeed, there is great debate over the issue of whether a camel has feet, hooves, or — God forbid — paws. If one considers this to be inconsequential, let me warn one, there is a deep epistemological abyss opening at one's — lets say — feet. Check your ropes, adjust your harness, ignite your headlamp, for down into the interpretive darkness we will descend. Let us see what illumination can be shed upon these Stygian pedi-puzzling depths.

Were one to examine closely the camel's (let us say "mobility extension" for purposes of discussion) mobility extension, one would find it is composed of two toes with hard, hoof-like nails. The two halves are joined by a leathery webbing which allows the mobility extension to spread and flatten as weight is brought to bear upon it. The design is complicated, but impeccable, enabling the camel to traverse sand effectively and silently for long distances.

By rights, the camel's mobility extension should be called — by combining the words "foot" and "hoof" — a "foof". For after all, what makes a thing a foot and what makes a thing a hoof? Some say that all paws, hooves, and feet are all just types of feet, the thing used for locomotion at the end of the leg. And yet, at some point, some feet become hooves, and others paws. Where is the line? Some will say that we know a paw when we see one, as we know a hoof when we see one. This is true. And yet the camel's foot is neither. It is clearly not a hoof, and clearly not a paw. Especially when we look at it.

If a foot is neither clearly a paw or hoof, is it right to merely call it a foot? After all, a camel's foot is certainly not like a human foot. Why would it have the same name when it is not the same at all? It is a new creation, made for a specific purpose.

I grew up on a dusty street — several streets, actually — in a city called Cochabamba, in a country called Bolivia. On average we inhabited a different house every couple years due to a simple but mysteriously unique financial maneuver — derived from ancient Roman law — called *anticrético*. Allow me to explain: It is very difficult to acquire legitimate, cost-effective financing in a country like Bolivia. Or, actually, in Bolivia. It is also difficult in a country like Bolivia (or, again, actually in Bolivia) to secure optimal rent for a given property. The *anticrético* solution is essentially that of a local property owner borrowing a sum of money from (usually) a foreigner, and, instead of paying that foreigner interest on that money, allowing the foreigner to live rent-free in (or on) one of the owner's vacant properties for a defined period of time — typically one or two years — followed by the property owner returning the original lump sum of money, and the foreigner subsequently vacating the property.

The beauty and symmetry of this transaction is that both foreigner and local property owner each have something of value the other desires for their own specific (and temporary) usage. The foreigner has a lump sum of money; the local property owner has a vacant house suitable for rent. In simply agreeing to exchange valuable commodities for a fixed length of time, they both in a sense gain something valuable for nothing. The foreigner gets to live rent-free for the fixed time period, and the local property owner gets to use an otherwise inaccessible sum of money interest-free for the same fixed time period. In the meantime, the foreigner has spent zero money on rent for the fixed time period, and the local property owner has been able to set in motion various business ventures which, without the foreigner's capital, would have otherwise been impossible. At the end of the fixed time period, the local property owner returns the principle to the foreigner. If he is unable to do so, the foreigner theoretically keeps the property, though this rarely transpires.

Why am I saying all this? One may have become aware without my being explicit — or even entirely intelligible — that the entire system of Bolivian *anticrético* is essentially built unwittingly upon the principle of the camel's foof. Who knew? And how is this possible in a land devoid of camels? Firstly, not all camelids are camels. Secondly, Bolivia has its fair share of camelids. The tension therefore between the two *anticrético* poles of balanced but opposing values creates a contingent attachment whose plasticity is of great performative worth in traversing Bolivia's difficult — but potentially productive — commercial terrain.

But I wanted to talk about dust, and possibly sand. Bolivian financial intricacies were only the motile mechanism used to approach the topic. Dust is not common where I now live. It is hardly an issue, as it rains much of the time. But my childhood was all about dust. In the house; on the street; in the truck; riding my bike; walking; hiking. Always dust. But not the same dust, for dust is less like pasta and more like prejudice. In one case, variety masks sameness; in the other, sameness masks variety. For example, I learned most household dust is mainly composed of dead human skin. Ashes to ashes; dust to dust, indeed. Street dust is different from trail dust. And jungle dust is different from mountain dust.

Dust, like sand, is only the pulverized remnant of some particular substance. And what is the difference between dust and sand, or even dirt? Grain size and source of substance, with the former generally functioning as the main determinant. (Dust particles are generally smaller than sand particles.) Is it true that all we are is dust in the wind, as the musical group, Kansas, once sang? (And which I can never listen to without thinking of a certain terraced — and occasionally dusty — property in the Bolivian city of La Paz?) No, of course not, for our substance transcends the conditions of our mortal existence. However, the lyric certainly contributed to a resonant, nostalgic, and allusive song. If one cares for such things.

My parents once bought me a pair of athletic shoes from a local shoe store near a plaza forested with date-bearing palm trees. (The trees have nothing to do with this tale, but I cannot think of that time — or those shoes — without them.) These shoes were very light, and had thick white soles which I was convinced were highly effective for navigating over — and upon — dust and sand, for how could they not be? I called them "sand shoes". My friends were very impressed, for they had never heard of "sand shoes" before, though in fact the style of shoe itself was quite common.

We were once hiking deep in the mountains when we came upon a dry river bed. Only scattered rocks and deep quicksand remained. Our path required us to cross this terrain. My friends said, "You must cross first, for you have sand shoes, and thus will be able to determine the best path upon which the rest of us may pass without sinking."

This made no sense whatsoever unless they were either stupid or indeed did not believe my shoes were sand shoes at all. For if they were — sand shoes, that is — how could they — my friends, that is — follow my path in any case? Their shoes would not be capable. And were sand shoes automatically also quicksand shoes? It was a very complicated situation. But there was nothing to be done but forge ahead, sand shoes or not. I simply walked and, by testing my steps as I went, found a path suitable for my friends. I had gotten in over my head, but thankfully did not get in over my head.

The camel's foof is a type of sand shoe. We know this for sure, unlike my equivocal childhood sand shoe. And the camel's foof can be regarded as a symbolic representation implicating us as Christers in this current age. There has been much talk lately of "de-wrathing" God. As if love could be love without consequence for evil. I suggest instead a "re-wrathing" of God, for it is the very tension between the two hard toes of God's love and God's wrath — both burning at the top of their energy (as G.K. Chesterton observes)[35] — which anchors the flexible leather strap of our being, enabling us to traverse the shifting, sinking sand of popular culture.

Are we God's feet? Are we God's hooves? Are we God's paws? None of these will do, for we are a new creation, metaphysical foofs, capable of things never before considered, but only if anchored to the poles of truth which allow our proper function. A rubber band cannot stretch without opposing forces. Likewise, we are stretched by God's love and wrath. Our faith is held in tension. But that very tension allows us to live. Otherwise we become brittle and ineffective, or soft and likewise ineffective.

God's love alone will not heal the morbidity of this universe, unless that love contains justice. A father without wrath is a father without love. One cannot purify water by bringing it to a consistent boil without heat. God's wrath is His love's balancing agent. We work out our faith in fear and trembling.[36]

Through the sand of this world's desert — and the dunes of this essay — the camel's foof has helped show us the way.

For the Christer, our *anticrético* Christ has accepted our souls in exchange for life. But the Master keeps our souls securely saved. He so chooses not to return them. And so we are forever gifted with life.

Christ, the loving but wrathful Messiah, is our sand shoe. Destined for the dust heap, we tread over the ashes of death, and rise on the pliant soles (and souls) of our new resilience.

For we are made more than dust and greater than sand.

We take form. We cohere. And we co-inhere.[37]

Or so I hear.

Pause and consider.

CHAPTER 10

ROOSTER

<u>PARAFABULON</u>

Once there was a great rooster who crowed even more than most. He was very proud.

When the dog barked, he said, "I will crow louder."

When the cow mooed, he said, "I will crow louder."

When the pigs oinked, he said, "I will crow louder."

When the donkeys brayed, he said, "I will crow louder."

When the lightning thundered, he said, "I will crow louder."

He said, "I will crow louder than any one or any thing at any time for any reason." And he strutted around the farmyard like a king.

One day it rained very heavily. The rain left many small pools of water gleaming in the sunshine as the clouds broke up and fled away into the distance.

The rooster glanced into one of these pools and was immediately transfixed by what he saw. He stepped into the pool of liquid, but his claws only served to muddy the waters, momentarily chasing the reflection away. He stared in amazement as the image returned. He could not look away. He stopped crowing. He stopped eating. He gazed upon the surface of the water for what seemed like days. He looked for so long hens became worried. In truth, his lack of crowing was more disturbing than all the crowing which had gone before, for a hen house with no crowing is like a well with no water.

Hens called a farm-wide meeting of all hens, young and old.

"Who will tell him that what he sees is only his own reflection?" they said, for they were afraid he would be angry.

"You," they said to a young one, "you will go and tell him."

So: young hen, not without some fear and trembling, went to the great rooster.

"Sir," she said, "that is only your reflection."

"I know," he said, "but do not say only."

RUMINATIO

It has been said — most likely by myself, for I am a simple man living a simple life — that it must require a remarkable degree of narcissism to enjoy acting or public speaking. Or perhaps a solid amount of sociopathy, possibly even a touch of psychopathy. But this may be saying too much and going too far for one not clinically licensed to make such assessments. Indeed, I have heard it said the secret to successful public speaking is to focus on specific individuals within the audience, not the group as a whole.

However, one can easily imagine the lack of interpersonal empathy and overweening megalomania it might require to subsume large numbers of individuals under the abstract entity referred to as a crowd. And one might even guess at what sort of moustache would prove suitable. *Selah*. (It goes without saying — though I am here saying it — that any account of mass manipulation is incomplete without at least some reference to Adolf Hitler.)

Søren Kierkegaard, the individualistic Danish "walking-philosopher" of spiritual inwardness, was keen on saying the crowd was untruth.[38] If, then, the crowd is untruth, what does that make the crowd's speaker? What else but untrue? How could the speaker's speech be anything but fabrication? The speaker can be to the crowd as the crow is to the rooster, for in the speaker the crowd finds its tongue. Indeed, the words "crowd" and "crow" are nearly identical, the differential "d" simply highlighting the crowd's persistent potential for a "declaimer". (But this sort of wordplay can only go so far before the clouds open and the rain falls, not to mention the fallout from lightning striking the literary tree under which one shelters.)

And yet one might say, "The Master himself spoke to crowds — was he then not to be trusted?" By no means. That is, by no means was he not to be trusted, for the Master sought solitude as one thirsting in the desert seeks water. He spoke out of necessity, not vainglory, for this is possible. He spoke out of love, not pride. For this too is possible. He spoke to the individual, not the crowd, for a gathering of individuals is not always a group, and individuals in a group are not always groupies.

So then: the speaker is the voice of the crowd, but not always. It is possible the opposite may be true — the voice against the crowd. Consider Moses, whom God chose — despite Moses having some manner of speech defect — to speak to the Israelites. Did I say *despite* a speech defect? Perhaps rather *because*, for it will always be known that such wisdom as Moses spoke came from God, not through his own eloquence. Indeed, perhaps one can be so wisdom-filled and self-forgotten that one overlooks oneself entirely, becoming a hollowed-out, self-excavated conduit of pure information flowing from a source divine. But I am talking about the Master and those who may follow him, for humility is required, and the word humble comes from the Latin "humus", ground, earth. For how can we be shaped unless we present ourselves as shapeable? How can adobe be fashioned without earth? How can a sand castle be sculpted without sand?

One may observe the potentiality of both pride and humility emanating from the speaker's perch. As has been said, not every soapbox carries soap, and not every speaker standing upon a soapbox is clean. Where then is the soap? Pause and consider. Each has their own gifts. It is easy to condemn another's gifts when one does not understand or possess them. Lord knows what I have suggested in satire has often been condemned as blasphemy. (Thank goodness for the invention of pseudonyms.)

But I am speaking of pride. And self-esteem. And what of self-esteem? Surely this cannot be a bad thing, one might say. And yet the reality is, at any given moment honesty requires us to admit we are a mess, no deserving candidates for esteem, and certainly not self-esteem. We may be less of a mess than previous iterations of ourselves, but we are certainly more of a mess than our future selves could be. The cult of self-esteem says we should be satisfied — even delighted — with our current selves. I find no evidence as to why this should be so, for it precludes the possibility of improvement. Indeed, we should be our own worst critics, requiring more and accepting less. For — as the sages of old have said time and time again — it is about the reals, not the feels.

In truth, one needs neither self-esteem nor other-esteem. We should esteem neither ourselves nor others, but God alone. What we truly require is non-esteem, to simply do what we do with modesty and, in humility, be what we should be in the Master, which suggests a wry, empathetic, consistently-improving-but-neverending dissatisfaction with our more than obvious shortcomings and those of others. For we as Christers have already shouldered our crosses and sacrificed our selves. Our only concern should be what to do with our personal mess in this world as part of Christerica, and how to do it.

Feeling good about ourselves has nothing to do with truth and love. None of us are what we could be, much less what we should be. Esteem, whether towards ourselves or to others, is a subjective mental game for those unwilling to live forthrightly. We must stand straightforwardly and face life squarely, orienting ourselves to the True Center of the encircling cosmos. We must constantly remember to forget ourselves, to calmly focus upon our work and work upon our focus, for there alone is worth, and even then only in Christ. We must have a sense of humor, and laugh at ourselves regularly, for we are immeasurable jokes, deserving of dunce caps, but undeservedly crowned with God's infinite love.

But then again, what of pride? And what of roosters? One beautiful summer day, we made plans to enjoy the city's seashore with our extended family. We parked several blocks from the beach and began to make our way on foot through the busy streets. But the streets were more than busy, for it turned out our plans coincided — and our path intersected — with the city's annual gay pride parade. Now, I have nothing against "gay" people per se, though as a Christer I do not share their moral convictions — or lack thereof — regarding certain lifestyle choices. Indeed, the Master is quite clear on what constitutes an appropriate sexual morality and an approved marital structure, and a Christer aims for what is believed to be the highest ethic. But not everyone is a Christer, and one has a right to do what one likes in the privacy of one's own bedroom. It is for God alone to sit in judgment. (And, perhaps, one's interior decorator.)

However, on this fine day, the privacy of the bedroom was not at issue, as was made abundantly clear by the very public and very naked approach of a rainbow-flag-waving, deeply tanned, "gay" gentleman. Fortunately, distracting from his full frontal microaggression — though not entirely mitigating its effect — was a pair of very nice white running shoes, which no doubt were a source of additional pride, for they looked as new and fresh as the skin above was leathery and dark.

But pride: what an odd standard under which to march, whatever the cause may be, for there are seldom parades for humility; there are no lofty banners for lowliness; no "sexual freedom" for those captive to Christ. Why pride? In truth, "sexual freedom" is only bondage to our fallen natures, but Christ's bondage is spiritual freedom. And it is for freedom we have been set free.

And lest this begins to sound somewhat judgmental, I must confirm that it is, for how does one follow a path without a pathway, a road without road signs? Indeed, who flies a plane without air traffic control? Well, most commonly, hijackers. But the free flight of the Christer is dependent on detailed instructions from the Tower, for without that Word, how shall we land safely? How will we come to ground if we cannot be firmly grounded? The Christer is less about wants, desires, or inclinations, and more about holiness and love, for I am talking about Christing. Indeed, love (or charity) "suffereth long, and is kind; charity envieth not; charity vaunteth not itself, is not puffed up, Doth not behave itself unseemly, seeketh not her own, is not easily provoked, thinketh no evil;

Rejoiceth not in iniquity, but rejoiceth in the truth; Beareth all things, believeth all things, hopeth all things, endureth all things."[39] "Sexual freedom" finds no place within this formulation, for it is often puffed up, often unseemly, and constantly seeking its own.

Some will argue that "love is love", but such a virtue-signalling formulation implies much but holds little content, for upon closer examination it is simply a meaningless and redundant tautological "deepity" dressed up as supposedly non-judgmental compassion. It is an empty container into which one can pour any emotional significance one desires and subsequently feel good about, though it addresses nothing and solves nothing. Indeed, one could counter such vacuity with the phrase "sin is sin", but one fears very few are familiar with such a word, or with the Master's own words, "go, and sin no more."[40] For who wants to talk about sin these days? As some will say, have we not transcended such terms and all the judgment and discernment they suggest, maybe even require?

However, as has been said, for the Christer, sexual desire is by no means a guide to proper conduct. It is filed in the appropriate folder for specific use. It is an application, not an operating system. Indeed, the will of the Master is our software, downloaded by the Spirit into the hardware of our beings, reformatting our souls for future upload into the heavenly realm. But I know very little about computers. Who knew a cloud could hold more than rain?

The world will do as the world does, no surprise to the

Christer, for those of the world are indeed worldly. Of more interest to myself at this moment — for I marvel at the strange influence of what may be called the lesser gods in human affairs — is the promotion of the word pride to endorse certain behaviors, pride being a far worse sin than any other — if such a thing can be said — for indeed, pride was (and is) the original sin. A "gay" lifestyle — as questionable as it might seem in relation to Christerical norms — certainly is a minor league player in comparison to pride, for pride is major league wickedness. To adopt pride as the character for such "sexual freedom" is like choosing nuclear weapons as a symbol for gun control, for pride is existentially and morally radioactive.

Pride is missing the mark, and by a wide margin. But it does not stop there. I noticed the crowing crowd, the proud crowd — which, you may remember (said Kierkegaard), is untruth — had also adopted the rainbow as a symbol for their "diverse" lifestyle. The rainbow, the very symbol of God's covenant with creation. (For that covenant extends to animals as well, even roosters.) The rainbow, whose seven colors may be seen to represent the seven Noahide laws, proscriptions against lustful and prideful conduct both being numbered amongst them, of all things. To use such symbolism as a way to promote the very modes of conduct it instantiates against is highly questionable indeed.

Noah's Ark is a symbol of our salvation in Christ. And that Ark, though full, was filled with very few. And those few were paired, male and female, for this is the way of life. For in the beginning God "created them male and female and blessed them".[41] And the rainbow itself can also be seen as a symbol of Christ, a spectrum of light, a royal coat of many colors. If, as it has been said, the rainbow is God's warbow, flung into the sky in such a way that the only arrows fired will thereafter fall upon himself, why does man insist upon firing them?

The confusion for many Christians regarding these matters — and I say Christians, for again, no Christer would ever consider such behaviour Christlike, as it does not aim in the right direction — derives from a mistaken conflation of their lives in Christ with the norms of the culture in which they are momentarily living, under the misapprehension of love, for who does not want to appear loving? However, when Christ says his kingdom is not of this world, he is already defining for us an alternate reality to that of these "nations" in which our mortal bodies are marking time and taking up space. For we truly are strangers in a strange land,[42] salt and light in a world of decay and shadow.

When I was a child, there were often times when I would injure myself, resulting in a cut or scrape. My mother would apply to the wound a stinging antiseptic liquid, for otherwise infection might easily set in, which could in turn lead to serious consequences. It hurt terribly when the medicine was applied. Nothing felt good about it. Yet it was good and right and necessary. And it was love.

Of course the world in its present form — which is passing away — will engage in worship and behavior at odds with Christer faith and belief — why would we possibly expect otherwise? But we are not the world or of the world. We are arks, Arks of the New Covenant. Each and every Christer is a Holy Ark, a Temple of the Living God, just as the earth is an ark for humans, Noah's ark an ark for animals, the Ark of the Covenant an ark for the holy objects of God. Indeed, the entire universe is an ark afloat upon the sea of the supernatural.

We in this world are used by the media we use. We are owned by what we own. Indeed, possessed by our possessions, trapped by our trappings, retooled by our tools. The very language we speak, this daily dictation, is our diurnal dictator, marching us to the tune of our own drumming. Our forms of construction are constructions of forms separating us from the natural world, ostensibly hiding our nakedness from each other and from a God from whom we can nevertheless not remain hidden. Everything is denial and avoidance, for we have been uprooted, and rootless we seek to find common ground in abstractions, rooted in nothing but air.

However, our engagement with the world is predicated upon our higher calling in the heavenlies. Our actions here are related to our higher reality. We are mirrors of the invisible. Our inner being is truly operating in another dimension, though we continue to be physically present here. To suggest, imply, or promote the need to acquire values — or acquiesce to values — derived from this lower reality is to simultaneously deny one's higher reality. As if the mortal could have more significance than the immortal. As if the branch were greater than the tree. As if the shadow could be more palpable than the real. We are of the Light. Therefore whatever shadows we cast in this land must be in conformity to that Light. Pause and consider. To a young mouse both cat and rooster appear monstrous. Better run than die discovering the difference.

God hates pride. God is at war with the proud. And yet the rooster, that proud barnyard animal, may be counterintuitively seen atop many a church steeple — indeed, I have seen it many times — for it crowed upon Peter's third denial of Christ, and it broke his spirit, leading to repentance and humility. The Master is our golden rooster. He breaks our spirit with his call, and the power of darkness which lies within. He, like the rooster, leads his henhouse to repentance and proclaims the new day. Is it any wonder then about the steeples? It is not.

But not being without sin myself, I merely cast stones into the air, whereupon they fall as often upon my own head as upon those of others. For I too must deny everything within myself which does not conform to the Master's will. That is the very nature of Christer faith. It matters not whatever urges or attractions beguile one, whether one has been born with them or somehow exposed to them along the way. Every one of us must contend with improper, immoral — or just plain silly — impulses and compulsions. This is obvious. The entire history of Christer life — indeed, all life — is that of an ongoing battle to sacrifice our natural inclinations — which are often unnatural (in light of the supernatural) — to a higher good.

Faith in Christ is not an exploration; it is a path. Faith in Christ is not an emergence; it is a conclusion. What many see as an "emerging" church may perhaps simply be one in the process of "submerging", one sinking under the waves whipped up by powerful winds of errant doctrine. This submergent church can only gradually sink into the flooding oblivion of secular culture, for it has not the orthodox sails or sturdy doctrinal gunwales to withstand the countervailing elements. The wintry winds and watery waves will inevitably erode its minimal distinctives, and the gates of hell may indeed prevail against it.

Seek and ye shall find, not seek and ye shall continue finding. There is something to be found, and something to be held, past which there is no finding, only aimless wandering. For if one leaves the orderly Christer path, one is simply left stumbling amongst the world's chaotic undergrowth. Tolkien's so-called "dark adventure"[43] may indeed await in either case, but the path — even in temporary darkness — provides direction, for to the pilgrim on the trusty trail — however rugged it might become — not all darkness is blindness.

When I was young I had a wooden board with skate wheels attached to it. This apparatus was literally called a skateboard. I believe similar devices are still being used in many countries for leisure and enjoyment. An interesting feature of a skateboard is the absence of brakes. A learner soon finds that stopping is the crucial skill to acquire. I learned a similar lesson when I chose to remove the brakes on my Bolivian bicycle. The logic behind this action was the stripping down of the bicycle into its constituent parts so as to paint the frame a free-spirited fluorescent orange.

The decision to not incorporate brakes into the bicycle's reassembly was the product of a youthful enthusiasm for a certain aesthetic of sporty minimalism. (I may even have been proud of it.) But the Andes Mountains are not amenable to such juvenile fancy. When my father and I — in the course of a long road trip through the Andean countryside — unloaded the bicycle from our vehicle at the top of a series of descending gravel switchbacks, I soon found as I sped down that dirt incline at increasingly greater rates that the parameters of reality are generally indifferent to fashion. My overly-optimistic hope of navigating the hairpin turns via some radical drifting method proved fruitless. I was forced in desperation to jam the sole of my shoe into the space between the rear tire and the bicycle's now-dusty fluorescent orange frame as a means of decreasing my unmanageable speed. In this way, I accomplished the complete destruction of my sole. (Those who have ears to hear, and so on. *Selah*.)

In mathematics, there is a statistical solution to various decision-making scenarios known as "optimal stopping". I am told it has something to do with 37%, and that is fair enough for those with sufficient understanding of numbers and the willingness to accept such odds. But I am more interested in the 100% of Christerica's optimal stopping, the 100% now. For now is the point of decision, the day of salvation. Today. Today is 100% the decision point of Christerica's optimal stopping.[44] The math, as they say, has been done.

Unbridled dialogue and endless conversation has no high Christerical value. Indeed, in many ways, Christerica halts dialogue and closes conversation, for Christ's "I am the way, the truth, and the life: no man cometh unto to the Father, but by me"[45] is more conversation stopper than conversation starter. It is, in truth, a *conversion* starter. Not a dialogue, but a (forgive me) "die-er's" log, a mortal diarist's first and final entry into the Book of Life, for talk is cheap but may cost all, even one's soul. In truth, it is conversion we seek, not conversation. And it is in conservation of that converting truth to which Christer conversation must inevitably converse.

For the Christer, life is sacrifice. What else could "take up your cross and follow me" possibly mean? The life of a Christer is sacrifice and responsibility in love, both of which require an engagement with norms of behavior which are not necessarily in keeping with our immediate desires. Whatever it is one desires, if it does not conform to the will of the Master, then, as a Christer, it is just too bad. Too bad for us. Too bad for him. Too bad for everyone. For it is exactly too bad. And we are about goodness.

Is this troublesome? Yes, it can be. Who would have assumed otherwise? As that old spiritual song declares, "Nobody knows the trouble I've seen, Nobody knows but Jesus". Indeed, I was forced to sing that song myself as a child. That was part of the trouble. And yet I took the message to heart, for undoubtedly the Master sees the heart.

So then: "When I was a child, I spake as a child, I understood as a child, I thought as a child: but when I became a man, I put away childish things. For now we see through a glass, darkly; but then face to face: now I know in part; but then shall I know even as also I am known."[46]

We are more than we think, and less than we thought. In the ancient tale of Snow White, her true beauty was in the magic mirror revealed. So too is our worth and unworthiness revealed in the Master's mirror. Self-reflection is not without value, especially for those without a mirror. And yet perhaps our judgments are not the best judgments, for we are more often funhouse mirrors in this carnival of life, reflecting only our own skewed reflections. Let us examine ourselves through the looking glass of the Master, for like Snow White we shall then see ourselves as we truly are. And then we will most likely cry, for we will inevitably appear grotesque. But there is nothing like a good cry, for the Master's mirror not only shows us what we are, but what we may become.

And when that becoming becomes — for it truly becomes us — then, and only then, shall we be what our being truly begs to be, the sum of the spectrum, root of the rainbow, wholly holy, and supremely grounded.

Pause and consider.

CHAPTER 11

SHEEP

<u>PARAFABULON</u>

Once there were sheep waiting for their master in a sheepfold. A stranger leapt over the wall amongst them.

"Here am I," he said.

"You are not our master," said the sheep, "for our master would have come through gate."

"I am your master," said the stranger.

"You are not our master," said the sheep, "for our master would have come through gate."

"I tell you truly, I am your master," said the stranger.

"You are not our master," said the sheep, "for our master would have come through gate."

"What must I do to show you I am your master?" said the stranger.

"You must come through gate," said the sheep.

"Consider," said the stranger, "if I am your master, the

sheepfold too is mine. The walls are mine and the gate is mine. Can I not enter however I choose?"

"Only gate," said the sheep.

"If I am your master," said the stranger, "do I not have the right to choose how I may come and how I may go?"

"Gate," said the sheep.

"So be it," said the stranger, and with one motion he leapt over the wall and into the next sheepfold.

"He did not go through gate," said the sheep.

Sounds of joy and celebration rose up from the next sheepfold.

"What goes on there?" said the sheep from the first sheepfold.

"We have found our master, and our master has found us," said the sheep from the next sheepfold.

"Did he come through gate?" said the sheep.

"We had no gate," said the sheep from the next sheepfold, "only walls."

"Then how could your master have come?" said the sheep.

"You were gate," said the others.

RUMINATIO

There was once a pharmacy in a village whose doors were open to the public for only very restricted hours. Its shelves were sparsely stocked, and what little there was in the way of effective medication was more costly than most could afford. And even then, the paperwork required to receive these scarce commodities was overwhelmingly complicated and burdensome, and generally restricted to a certain class of people who had lived in the village for many years, and who could afford to employ experts in the filing and submission of the appropriate documentation.

Meanwhile, the poor and unlettered majority had to make do with various unreliable folk medicines, dreadful home brews, and noxious poultices composed of the strangest and most pungent ingredients one could imagine, collected from the farms, forests and fields thereabouts.

One day a man claiming to be the pharmacy owner's son appeared in the village to proclaim a new medicine, one he alone could dispense, one that did not depend upon a physical pharmacy. It would no longer matter whether the pharmacy doors were opened or closed, whether the shelves were well-stocked or not, whether a fee charged or free of charge.

"All one must do," said the owner's son to the people of the village, "is believe in me, ask in my name, and one will be dispensed the medicine one needs to live."

"What is this medicine?" the villagers asked.

"It is my flesh and my blood," said the pharmacy owner's son, and so saying, he emptied the pharmacy and closed its doors. (Is this too obvious? Even so, most bread is not made without flour.)

There was amazement on one side and outrage on the other, for such a thing was unheard of, a thing beyond anything every dreamt of or previously imagined in that small village.

"What sort of sorcery is this?" said those with previous access to the pharmacy. "Let us make him this year's scapegoat." For they had a yearly practice of designating a known criminal to bear the sins of the community and to be destroyed along with them at a far distance as a propitiation to the gods. Therefore they beat the owner's son and left him for dead beyond the edge of the village.

But lo and behold, he returned, alive and well, maintaining his previous offer. Many were rightly overjoyed, and more than willing to believe, and more than willing to call upon the name of the owner's son, for they were truly sick, poor, and uneducated, and were fully convinced that boar's grease, horse urine, goat testicles, bat wings, pulverized rat, naturally scented clysters, and the like were not consistently producing the healing they so desired.

The scapegoaters were not so keen. They asked, "How could something given for free be of any value? After all, who gives precious jewels to a beggar, or fine gold to a herdsman?" And they truly suspected the man claiming to be the owner's son of not only being an impostor, but also a dangerous magician and sorcerer, for how else does one heal of such wounds and return from the dead?

Indeed, they refused to call on the name of the owner's son, or to eat of his flesh and drink of his blood, for how could such a thing even be possible? Surely, they thought, this was madness. They themselves reopened the pharmacy, stocking the shelves in the way they saw fit. They set up barricades, guards, more paperwork than before, and even instituted more restricted hours.

But the poor villagers did believe in the owner's son, and they did call on his name, and they did eat of his flesh and blood, for this is only possible with those who believe, and who therefore have the secret knowledge of its meaning.

In this way, the dying lived, and the living died, for not everyone accepts what is free, especially when it costs tradition. Who eats Christ's flesh and Christ's blood? Only the Christer who understands its meaning, for the Kingdom of God cannot be inherited by flesh and blood, but only by those worshipping in spirit and in truth.

For we too, like the villagers above, are living in a time when prescriptions and dispensations have been turned upside down, and perhaps even inside out. The earthly pharmacy remains partially open, but compromised. The heavenly pharmacy, though uncompromising, is fully open. And Christ is the only true *pharmakon*, a Greek word whose meaning suggests not only medicine, but scapegoating as well, and that which can either be remedy or poison. For if Christ is the true *pharmakon* — the eternal scapegoat and prescribed life-saving medicine — it is only ingesting the appropriate dosage which saves. We must consume the entire thing, flesh and blood, and perhaps even bone. Anything else produces death, for its conviction is poison to the unbeliever. Ingestion in the believer aids holy digestion; partial ingestion in the unbeliever effects unholy indigestion. I myself prefer the holy sort of digestion, for as the ancient sages say, regularity promotes godliness, as that which obstructs in one part may obstruct in another. *Selah*.

Some will say such medicine is a crutch, as if this were a valid criticism of Christer belief. And yet a crutch is exactly what is needed if one requires a crutch. And Christerica's crutch is God's "crutching" (trimming) our spiritual hindquarters to prevent the Devil's fly-strike, for indeed the Accuser is referred to as the Lord of the Flies, and will kick us in the butt. But I will not push that metaphor any further, for sheep driven too recklessly may stumble over a cliff and injure themselves, or wander into the jungle, where they will be preyed upon by many a wild beast without any recourse to actual or metaphorical salvation.

But enough woolgathering: if one believes in the salvation offered by the risen Christ to every person alive, one is a "dispensationalist" of one kind or another, call it what one wills. For to not believe in this current "dispensation" of the life-saving medicine which is the grace of God in Christ, is to deny the very thing which is able to make one a Christer. For it is not acknowledging the historical figure of Christ which makes one a Christer, neither is it praising his wisdom, but rather believing and consuming the holy pharmaceutical dispensed. Otherwise there is no Christerica. And where would that leave us? Sheep without a shepherd, penned in and penned out. But thanks be to God, we have been dis-penned. The gates are open. The walls are down. This is indeed a dis-pen-sation. We are out, and in outing, we are in.

My local pharmacy has a scale with a "tare" button which — when pressed — zeroes out the reading activated by the placement upon it of an empty container. Thus, only the subsequent contents are measured. In a similar manner, salvation in Christerica can be described as our being "tared". That is, the sinful weight of our being zeroed out, dispensed with. The slate is wiped clean. And subsequent measurement only reflects the weight of glory deposited upon us by the dispensation of our Redeemer's grace.

I am fascinated by — and indeed have various books displaying — all the charts, graphs, and timelines of the peculiar movement called "American Dispensationalism". In a similar manner, I am fascinated by the geometric forms and decorative designs of a Muslim mosque, or the beautiful stained glass and marble statuary of a Roman Catholic Gothic cathedral. These aesthetic components, though generated in some manner by the particular beliefs in question, are not a proof of that belief's truth, but neither are they a negation, for that is hardly the point at this level of resolution. They are simply marvellously, aesthetically pleasing in themselves — as with many a visual art form — regardless of their underlying truth claims or existential assumptions. Indeed, I have seen polluted, mud-filled canals whose oily surfaces coruscate with the most beautiful colors under the activating brilliance of the Andean sun.

But there is a difference between "Dispensationalism" as a comprehensive overlay of thought — with all its prophecies and predictions, its Gogs and Magogs — and the acknowledgement of the present dispensational nature of Christerica. In the same way excessive Mariolatry in some streams of Roman Catholicism does not negate the truth that Mary, the mother of Jesus, was certainly a very special woman in her own way, "American Dispensationalism" as a movement does not negate the true dispensational nature of Christerica.

Rather, Christerica manifests an agile dispensationalism which, like a well-fashioned sail, is supple and open enough to encompass powerful gusts of errant dogma, yet rigid and structured enough to maintain direction in the rough seas of doctrinal confusion. This well-balanced ship of faith enables thereby an effective means of spiritual transport on either the starboard tack of free will or the port tack of determinism, for the course has been charted; the Head has confirmed the heading; the mast of the Cross balanced with the keel of the Resurrection. But these are deep waters, and I am only a simple painter. However, mixing metaphors on the page is not so different from mixing mediums on the canvas.

Pause and consider: Christerica as we know it did not exist

before the death and resurrection of Christ. When, then, did Christerica begin? When did gentiles and Jews alike begin to enter into Christerica together? Somehow that transition had a lot to do with that man in transition, Paul, formerly Saul of Tarsus. And not only Paul. But still, lets talk about Paul, for he is unavoidably dominant in the collection of books entitled the New Testament, though he is not worthy — as he himself vouches[47] — to be called an apostle after his early persecution of the Church of God.

There is no question Christerica — and historical Christianity in general — is largely "Pauline" in our understanding, though Christic in nature. Christ himself raised Paul up to communicate this unique outpouring of God's spiritual grace upon the gentiles. Christ is at the center, but Christ speaking through Paul is a powerful lens through which we may view our current relationship with Christ. The earliest manuscripts of the New Testament reveal themselves to be Pauline. And in truth, throughout the entire Bible — so far as I am aware (though I am no scholar) — the word "spiritual" is used almost exclusively by Paul. Surely this must signify something noteworthy. If Christerica were a piece of jewelry — let us say a ring — the Pauline construction could be the setting, and Christ the gemstone. Knowledge of the structure is transmitted through Paul, but the point and focus of the structure is Christ. And let us even say it is a wedding ring, for after all, the Church is the Bride of Christ.

If that is getting too mystical, worry not, for it is somehow true all the same. We are talking about spiritual realities, after all, and after all, Christ did not provide our interpretive lens in his own words. He wrote nothing, nothing at all. And why would he? His work was not yet finished. Everything we think we know about Christ comes through his early followers. The only words of Christ we are aware of have been transmitted through followers and witnesses.

Indeed, the Master's last word is exactly Saul of Tarsus, raised up — kicking and screaming, so to speak — as the Apostle Paul, to be the main interpretive lens through which we view Christ's ultimate reality and that of the Body of Christ in this present moment. We too easily read Christianity back into the Judaism of Christ. Many are conflicted regarding this, for they rightly want to speak only of Christ. They attempt to give Paul due credit by damning with faint praise. "He was a religious genius!" they say, happily praising and condemning in the same breath. After all, what else can one say if one wishes to acknowledge Paul's overwhelming importance, but deny his spiritual and interpretive authority?

When some Christians say, "I don't know about that crazy Paul...", they are not realizing what they believe about Christ is exactly the message given Paul and his subsequent understanding of the dispensation of grace to all men under Christ. They are cutting off the branch upon which they stand, grafted in to the tree of God's working with the Chosen People. But they are not Jews. They are (or should be) Christers. Which means they are on the branch. And should be overjoyed they are on the branch. Indeed, they are the branch. Who in their right mind would cut it off?

After all, one must understand, Jesus was a Jew talking to Jews. Only in retrospect do we apply his words to ourselves. When reading what we call the Bible, none of the words contained therein were written directly to any of us. We simply appropriate the ones we feel are most applicable to us at this time in God's revelation. It is an easy thing to discern our exemption from Old and New Testament animal sacrifice, for we are clearly not Jews of the Old Temple paradigm. However, few seem well able to discern much beyond this, for much of Christianity is a confused scrabbling after the contents of the *piñata* of both Testaments broken open by those seeking spiritual treats. But a Christer is more exact than that, more mature, more focussed. A Christer worships in the spirit and the truth which Christ spoke towards, and which was more fully revealed in the letters of Paul, who still was trying himself to discern the praxis for the gentile believer in Christ. Many have asked me, what exactly then is a Christer? Can you be more clear? For it seems I am understood to speak in a confusing manner. My reply is generally very simple, and perhaps surprisingly traditional, even orthodox:

"I believe in God, the Father almighty, creator of heaven and earth. I believe in Jesus Christ, God's only Son, our Lord, who was conceived by the Holy Spirit, born of the Virgin Mary, suffered under Pontius Pilate, was crucified, died, and was buried; he descended to the dead. On the third day he rose again; he ascended into heaven, he is seated at the right hand of the Father, and he will come to judge the living and the dead. I believe in the Holy Spirit, the holy catholic Church (*that is, Christerica, not the "Roman" one*), the communion of saints, the forgiveness of sins, the resurrection of the body, and the life everlasting. Amen."

This may sound familiar to some. And well it should, for it is more commonly known as the Apostles' Creed, and is nearly two thousand years old. (Not including my italicized parenthetical interpolation.) There is very little for a Christer to disagree with there.

However, I will not tread this path much farther at this time for it ramifies greatly, and sheep will follow the ram, even into foreign fields. Enough to proffer contemplative fodder for those who wish to mull over such things in their spare time, for such provender can only be presented. Indeed, it is silage providing roughage only if eaten, and such roughage, though perhaps momentarily intestinally violent, ultimately soothes the bowels and promotes spiritual health.

For a foolish peace may cause more harm than a just war, and an earthly cross never disappoints, for its promise is death, and this is indeed what it delivers.

Bear, then, the cross of the Master, for it alone bears us as sheep to our predestined fold.

The pen may be mightier than the sword, but the sword may yet cleave open the walls of the pen, to find written there the Words of the Master, cutting both ways.

Pause and consider.

CHAPTER 12

GOAT

PARAFABULON

A goat climbed amongst the rocks and high places. The cliffs were where he roamed.

He was not afraid to fall, for he was not even aware that such a thing were possible.

He was made for heights. And heights, it seemed, were made for him.

"I will go where I want," said the goat, "and I will eat what I eat, and I will say what I feel."

The animals on the valley floor did not trust the goat.

"Why will he not come down amongst us and live as we do?" they said. "Why is he so high?"

Indeed, none of the animals would have been able to climb the rocks in the way of the goat.

One day the goat saw in the distance a band of hunters approaching, for as usual he was well up on the cliff and could see to the horizon and beyond.

"Beware," said the goat to the animals on the valley floor, "a band of hunters approaches."

"Why would you say something so hateful?" said the animals on the valley floor.

"It is not hateful," said the goat, "it is true. Hunters approach."

"You are proud and will not live like us or say the things we want to hear," said the animals on the valley floor.

"I am not proud," said the goat, "I can simply climb on rocks and in high places and see to the horizon."

The ones who believed the words of the goat fled and were saved. The rest were captured and secured with ropes.

As they were led away by the hunters, the captured ones said, "It just goes to show — never trust a goat."

RUMINATIO

I have seen many goats in my travels. But also many sheep. I have observed that sheep are gentle, often fearful. They are flocked, but they also flock. Following, of course, follows. Social they are and docile they be. (Though for rutting rams I will not vouch.)

Goats, on the other hoof, seem fearless. Independent, devious, and willful. Goats have personality. And gentle they may not be. It is no wonder — as in the preceding parafabulon — that sheep are wary of goats. Indeed, a so-called "Judas goat" can be trained to lead herds of sheep to the slaughter, or to lead hunters to wild goats which the hunters wish to eradicate. I see no reason why this cannot be seen as a warning for the Christer as well. For as the Scriptures say, "there be some that trouble you, and would pervert the gospel of Christ. But though we, or an angel from heaven, preach any other gospel unto you than that which we have preached unto you, let him be accursed.."[48]

This is all well and good, but how — one may ask — does one identify a "Judas goat", for by its very nature it deceives? To begin, have a firm stance. Get low on your feet, but high in your view. Be alert. Do not follow and do not lead. Look. Listen. Pray. Know what you believe, and what has been believed. And be ready to give warning, for the human Judas goat will ask two things: believe a new thing, and follow. So then: do not believe a new thing, and do not follow. For a Christer follows only Christ.

What shall we say then, must even a goat not trust a goat? By no means, for not all goats are Judas goats, and not all sheep are sheep. Some goats may speak, and speak well. But beyond these interspecies and intraspecies trust issues, I have found that both sheep and goats have strangely slitted eyes, which I must confess bother me greatly, for I do not understand them. (And I wish to speak of vision.)

I am told the ovine and hircine horizontal pupils allow for

improved wide-angle predator detection while preventing sunlight from bleaching perception. This may even be true, for they are indeed prey animals. Strange that I, a predator — for all humans are predators (though, curiously, we see ourselves more often as prey) — am powerfully disquieted by them. I cannot look into those slitted eyes and make a human connection. They are alien to me, impenetrable. Them with their uncanny eyes. Who will save me from their unearthly reproach?

And yet, is it unearthly? Part of the problem with goats, it seems, is they are exactly too earthly and earthy. Their wild, hairy, and unruly behaviour has always been metaphorically hedonistic, satyrical, perhaps even diabolical. How often have we seen this portrayed? More than once, my friends, more than once. And not without reason.

However, it must be said, goats are not considered unclean in the Biblical tradition. They, along with sheep, are ceremonially clean.[49] In fact, for eons gone by, the Yom Kippur rite of purification on the Day of Atonement called for two goats, one — the purification goat — to be sacrificed upon the altar, and another — the scapegoat — to be solemnly burdened with the nation's sins and sent out into the wilderness. The purpose of this rite was obviously two-fold. (Wait...fold. Two folds. Sheep, goats; Jew, gentile; right, left; older sibling supplanted by younger sibling. And wait... atonement. I once heard the interim youth pastor of a small church deconstruct the word into "at-one-ment". He is now working as a barista. But nevertheless, Christ: one sacrifice, two functions; two peoples, one body. And what great trickery, for Christ our sacrifice and scapegoat has not only provided for the cleansing of the world and everything in it, but has simultaneously drawn the Accuser away — for the Accuser is drawn to sin as a fly to dead meat — into the eternal wasteland by the Master's death, and by the Master's resurrection has been left holding the bag by which he will be weighted down forever. Such is the heavenly bait and switch.)

But perhaps I myself have wandered too deeply into that parenthetical interpretive wilderness, although it has been said, the wider the landscape, the greater the view, and a goat on a cliff may see farther than a sheep on the ground. And again, not all movement is progress, and yet — as J.R.R. Tolkien observed — not all who wander are lost.[50] We lock our selves inside interpretive rooms at our peril, for within four walls there is no view except of the walls themselves. (And the floor. And, okay, the ceiling.) No amount of stained glass will sufficiently translate the heavens, but a step outside the door may open a world of perception, not to mention access to fresh air.

So then: there is something about eyes and vision which is far-reaching in its reality and symbolism. It has been said the eyes are windows to the soul. I myself have never seen a soul through anyone's eye-windows, though a well-rounded pupil reveals a diminutive reflection of myself. Indeed, the eyes of others may be partial windows to our own souls, for we see as we are seen.

Our Heavenly Scapegoat has opened the doors of our perception to a perspective of much higher resolution — a goatscape, if you will — for previously we viewed our existence at a much lower resolution. But we are not jpegs — as those with computer literacy have taught me — though such lossy compression may be useful for daily simplification. Indeed, we Christers are not rastered at all, prone to image distortion and pixelation. We are vector files, retaining our true resolution and eternal proportions at any size. Unchanging and unchangeable, we adapt and reform as needed with no loss of resolution.

Now our goatscape renders a broader vision as well, the better with which to detect predators — both visible and invisible — wishing to stalk our souls. But not only souls and not only predators. We have integrity as individuals. For the seeker must avoid prejudice, as blindness may obscure the hand of a friend as well as that of an enemy.

And just so, as with goats on a cliff, we have been made self-aware, balanced, alert. We have taken up our responsibilities and are keen to discern the many levels of reality composing the layer cake of life. We shout warnings if we must, and encouragement also, for we no longer live low resolution lives where nothing resolves. Certainly we still see through a glass darkly, but at least we have begun to open the blinds.

After all, it is not about our life. It is about Christ's life in us. Or our life in Christ. Either way, we are defined by the Master. That is our definition. And it is a high definition. We have constantly sought better existential resolution. We have needed corrective lenses. In Christ we have found the highest, most advanced spectacles. And we in turn have been made spectacles. Indeed, fools for Christ. But make no mistake, they — and we — are corrective. Our function is to lens, not obscure. We are Christ-prescription eyewear, not shades. We do not block the Son, for he is the light we see by. Pause and consider.

There was a time when I found myself playing point guard for a basketball team touring various cities, towns, and villages in South America. We were a band of young Christers — optimistic, prankish, and overly energetic — sent out to spread the message of the Master's grace and peace across the heathen hardwood (or pagan concrete, or faithless dirt, as circumstances warranted). We somehow hoped to achieve this by playing smothering defense, crushing offense, and speaking at half-time about the love of Christ. Our cross-grained efforts were not entirely winsome, but at least we were trying.

Our coach was a strong proponent of the idea that basketball was played off the court between games as much as on the court when the clock was ticking and the stands were full. In other words, the game was always in progress — not just on game day — whether in basketball or in life, for mental preparation and physical training were as essential as game strategy and performance.

He had a trick metal vase filled with water which he used in his presentations to represent the diminishing power of life without the Master, for he would progressively spill the contents onto the ground in the course of his discourse until the vase seemed empty and — apparently — not a drop remained. Such was the picture of a life without Christ. But then, upon a powerfully delivered proclamation of the promised fulness of life in Christ, he would once again upend the vase and a torrent of water would miraculously pour out.

It was all very effective upon first contemplation, but after innumerable viewings of this hydro-pneumatic trickery, the effectiveness certainly decreased over time for many of us youthful basketeers. However, his point was clear and it sharpened our vision. For if one's vision is weak, how can one play basketball? Or, indeed, see penetratingly into the distance? Or, indeed, live the Christer life?

I once read a book — and subsequently viewed the motion picture (which did very little justice to the book, not surprisingly) — based upon the experimental, government-sanctioned activities of a covert group of American servicemen recruited for their supposed psychic abilities.[51] As part of their efforts to weaponize their latent powers, they had procured access to "Goat Lab" — an apparently derelict shed secretly stocked with a number of military goats (de-bleated in the interests of confidentiality) used for surgical training — and were attempting to stop (maybe even burst) their hearts via telekinetic power alone.

Many questions immediately arise, the one most germane to

our discussion being: why goats? And the question is answered in part because, in the military's case, it was believed a goat was the animal with which it was least likely for a soldier to form an emotional bond. Goats are an idea of "the other" in material form. This is their metaphorical significance. And in the case of Goat Lab, only one goat dropped dead in the course of these quasi-clandestine "Black Op" experiments, but the agent involved simultaneously developed heart complications of his own. Thus we see that harming others may indeed harm ourselves in a similar measure, though this lesson remains to be taught so well as others.

Another question which might arise is: why does all this seem so comical? For we instinctively think: of course, goats — what else? Goats and comedy, maybe even satire (for the word satire partially derives from satyr, that wild, capricious mythological man/goat hybrid), have always gone together like cashmere and sweaters. The goat is the butt of a joke as often as it butts the joker.

In sporting terms, the player (or fan) responsible for a loss has been traditionally referred to as a goat. Indeed, I have seen this myself. And who can forget baseball's infamous Curse of the Billy Goat, which the Chicago Cubs were only able to break after seventy-one years. That is no joke. At least not for them and their fans. For everyone else, well, we all have our own sense of humor.

However, words being changeable as they are (as mentioned

in the Preface), a new denotation for the word "goat" has arisen. In like manner to the death and resurrection of Christ, the word "GOAT" — which formerly expressed that which was lowest — has now risen to mean the highest, an acronym for "Greatest Of All Time". Salvation indeed can occur in the most unlikely circumstance and location, for if even a goat can undergo such metaphorical transformation, then something transcendent is truly afoot. Indeed, as has been said, the last shall be first, and the first shall be last.

In ancient Greek a "tragedy" was a "goat-song", and a "comedy" a "party-song". But in Christ, what starts out as a "goat-song" becomes a "party-song", that is, a comedy, a story with a happy ending. It is goat-song all the way to the tomb, but party-song all the way out.

The goat is a comedian, a trickster (Jacob uses goatskins to trick Isaac,[52] and goats again to later trick Laban)[53], a Kierkegaardian individual. And yet comedy, in the end, is no joke. For it is often the outsider, the King's jester, who can see most clearly and give voice to dangers the sheep may not see. For sheep are not adventurous and are disinclined to scale dangerous cliffs or to explore distant lookouts, and if the emperor has no clothes, who but a fool can tell him?

So what shall we do with all this? Let us see if, like a well-worn deck of cards, we can shuffle these ideas and deal them in some semblance of a reasonable hand.

Atonement theories abound. What did Christ dying on the cross — and rising from the dead — actually accomplish?

Some say a victory over the powers of evil. Others say victory over death. Others say it satisfied God's wrath against human sinfulness. And yet others speak of the scapegoating mechanism. Goats to the left, and sheep to the right, indeed, but card shuffling generally involves both hands.

So then, what if we stack the deck? What if we become sheep with just enough goat shuffled in to enable us to follow Christ in the appropriate manner? For he too — though a lamb led to the slaughter, a sacrificial ram — is our substitutionary scapegoat, goat enough to carry our sins to as far as the east is from the west.

To sing the song of our selves is to sing a goat-song, for that is a great tragedy. But to sing the song of the Master is to sing a party-song, for we celebrate life in the true GOAT. And the true GOAT is a buck, and he says the buck stops here.

Upon this, let us ruminate. For illumination the truly ruminant seek.

And redemption — in its ceaseless iterations — is our rumen, the infinite room in which we are digested as we digest, masticating the Master's feed each in our own wild yet trusting way.

Pause and consider.

CHAPTER 13 + 14

GRASSHOPPER / ANT

<u>PARAFABULON</u>

Once there was a grasshopper who lived freely under the sun, enjoying every minute of every beautiful day. But the weather changed and the sun stopped shining and the air grew cool-and-crisp and there was no more food.

The grasshopper met an ant who had worked all through the bright, warm, good days, filling its storehouse with food for the coming winter.

"I am hungry," said the grasshopper.

"I am not surprised," said the ant, "for I have seen you jumping and eating and playing all summer long as I worked my way through the fields, collecting every bit of food I could find."

The grasshopper sadly turned to leave.

"Where are you going?" said the ant.

"I do not know," said the grasshopper. "I am lost."

"Why are you lost?" said the ant.

"Because I have no food and I do not understand it."

"Did you not think to collect it?"

"I was overwhelmed by the beauty of the field."

"What is beauty?" said the ant.

"Oh!" said the grasshopper, "it is the movement of the sun, the stars, the moon, the wind, the forest; it is the field in all its color; it is life in all its texture; it is all and everything all the time!"

"And could you teach me more of this beauty?"

"Oh, yes," said the grasshopper. "Of course!"

"You may eat of my provisions," said the ant.

"I may?" said the grasshopper, overwhelmed.

"Yes — I owe it to you," said the ant.

"Why?" said the grasshopper.

"Because," said the ant, "I am sure that I have — in some small, inexplicable manner — fed upon your joy all summer, and I will now continue to feed upon this beauty you have found — if you will share it with me — for it is food I would not know how to collect. So then: my prevision and your vision will be our shared provision."

RUMINATIO

One perceives the moral of the preceding parafabulon immediately, for it is as obvious as the sun in the sky or an anthill upon the plain. Or indeed, a grasshopper in the kitchen. There is truly no requirement for one such as myself to comment further. However, this makes little difference, for I would speak of beauty all day long. And for most of the night. Sometimes I do, for the Grasshopper Criterion is strong within me. What is the Grasshopper Criterion, one may ask? It is the irrepressible impulse towards an appreciation of beauty. It is attention to the ordinary, which — in almost every respect — is extraordinary.

There is no end to beauty, for like an onion, it is built into this cosmos layer upon lovely layer, unto its very core. And the core of beauty is the dwelling place of God, the source of all. At least I like to think so, for how else would we recognize such beauty as beauty if there were not such a thing as original beauty? (My lachrymal fluids run even now at the thought, for the cherubim shield from mine eyes none of the Creator's incandescent synthasial glory. But enough about onions.)

Long ago I authorized the automatic personal renewal of my subscription to the following vocational credo: "Making things beautiful, and making beautiful things (or at least trying)". For I am an embellisher. It is in truth my vocation, my calling. (That is, if I have heard aright.) What is an embellisher? One who embellishes. (I have always found it secretly — and publicly

— amusing to define a word by using a variation of the very word in question, ever since a classmate of mine in Grade Five — or was it Six? — tried this ruse in all seriousness, for he was always wont to give an answer first despite provisional ignorance, such was his desperation to be praised by the teacher and envied by his peers. To his blushing shame, it did not work in the way he intended. His definition was ill-defined, in turn defining him as definitely ill, for he certainly looked unwell after the teacher's acerbic rejection. My how we laughed — laughed ourselves sick. But enough about tears.)

Simply speaking, to embellish means to make something beautiful. Or more beautiful. How? In whatever manner best suits the thing in question, for to me genuine embellishment does not lie in lying, but in a sort of genuine decorative advocacy. That is, its truth lies in its artisanal augmentation without dissemblance in regards to an underlying authenticity. For instance, if I paint a pillar made of plastic, wood, or drywall to look like sandstone or marble, I am not claiming it to be actual marble — though indeed many are fooled into thinking so — I am merely giving it the appearance of beauty to which it could never aspire in its natural, unfinished state. Is it a lie? No — it is a true fiction, for it expresses a level of potential beauty which the item does not currently possess. Does this mean anything? I think it does, for all fiction can be a means of revealing truth, and all words are a sort of fiction which — like calculus approximating the area under a curve — functionally approaches the curve of reality without ever quite fully reckoning it.

Embellishment can reach a level of such flawless perfection that the object very nearly becomes the subject of an alchemical transformation. But not quite, for the ancient practice of alchemy — that strange protoscientific mixture of mysticism and chemistry — has never been able to produce its philosopher's stone, for the stone has been rolled away, and embellishment stops short of the tomb. Only the Master can truly change our very nature. But this is no longer embellishment. This is transcendent transfiguration, the only alchemy truly possible.

For earthly alchemy is a dreamer's blunderland, and no less appealing for all that. Even the great scientist Isaac Newton could not resist its charms, spending years manipulating ovens, retorts, cucurbits, and alembics to little avail. But we can easily forgive him this personal mania — after all, who does not like to slave over cucurbits and alembics? — for he simultaneously did a few other things, like invent the aforementioned calculus, describe (and name) gravity, develop the Three Laws of Motion, discover the color spectrum, and so on. Indeed, upon further consideration, perhaps we should give alchemy the same credit due all fictional representations which lead to technological advancement, for one could argue the smartphones which inhabit our palms were inspired by the imaginative protocols of the televisual production known as Star Trek. This is only one example. One could suggest many more. Like author Jules Verne and modern submarines. Or the Star Wars movie franchise and light sabers. (Patience, my friends, patience.) It seems imagination always precedes invention and implementation.

The Scriptures relate the incredibly dramatic story of Joseph and his coat of many colors. As a painter, I like the color of many coats. And yet both have a share in beauty. If I were to embellish upon the Biblical witness, I might suggest Joseph's coat of many colors could be the same one Christ wore many years later, the same garment over which the soldiers cast lots while Christ was dying upon the cross. Or I could suggest that we ourselves, the nations of the world, are the coat of many colors our Savior humbly wears. These are all embellishments, faux finishes, creative insights (or possibly oversights, misguided interpretive faux pas), decorative applications with declarative implications. They need not be factual so long as they make no definitive claim to fact, and yet they may also be true in the same way that my painted pillar may actually be marble beneath its painted finish (and sometimes is), or speak a truth about marble which the suboptimal substrate could not tell itself. For it is often the case that those who have something to say have not the words to say it, and those with the words to say something have nothing to say.

Indeed, both fact and fiction are rendered believable by the imagination, as we would not be able to apprehend truth or beauty otherwise, for imagination is the power to understand that which cannot be seen, and to see what cannot be understood. The word itself says what it does. And just as Christing is a verb, so is imagining, for it is the faculty of our mind which produces the imaginings we need to augment our understanding.

For if we live in a cloud of unknowing, it is only because we are the precipitate in that cloud. If there were no cloud, we would not only know nothing, but would cease to exist. Our unknowing is the precondition for our knowing. Existence is limitation, but it is also precipitation. We rain on our own parade, for there would be no parade without the rain of consciousness.

Indeed, reality is a very slippery entity, for it is examined with tools of its own elusive nature. Objectivity seems truly out of reach. And yet we cannot resist this existential exploration, for it seems we are supernatural beings foreshortened temporarily by this seemingly material construct. Is this earth a prison? A form of transportation? Theater for the angels? An arena of war? A supremely dramatic game? Is it a Child's plaything? And why should we care? Yet we do! We cannot help ourselves. We generate story after story, reflecting, imaging, imagining, considering, reconsidering. But we cannot see under; we cannot see around or behind. And indeed, there may be no under or around or behind. But we are forever haunted by this notion of meaning. Our obsession with narrative is testimony to the operative reality of cause and effect. So what is the cause? It must be — must Be — some sort of preexistent Being. A Be-ing. So why then are we here? Be-cause. Maybe that is explanation enough.

An ant in a small box may come to realize the limits of that box fairly quickly, and dimly realize it is trapped, but at some conceptual horizon of enlargement, the box will become too big for the ant to functionally determine its limits, thereby imparting a notion or perception of limitlessness. Perhaps the same could be said for humans. We require, minimally, a universe as vast as the one we inhabit for it not to seem boxed in. (Even though we are boxed in.) We feel space and time are sufficient to the idea of a life lived in freedom. This, of course, is an illusion, for in truth we do not even escape this earth, our bodies recycled continually into the elements. Our current global mapping has only served to show us how lost we truly are, for we can now clearly see there is nowhere to go. There is no mystical terra incognita any longer, only an easily viewable terra cognita. What then?

I have heard certain sports fans refer to their team's long-term strategy as one of trusting "The Process". Indeed, such a nickname can devolve upon a key player who embodies the notion inherent in that strategy. In like manner, Christerica has a winning long-term strategy most obviously embodied in the figure of the Master. Christ is "The Process". And if we trust The Process, it will pay as we play, for the earthly playoff will result in unearthly payoff, and this spirit factory, this existence refractory, will through us refract, its mystery cracked. And so we act.

A true artist then, if anything, is one who is sensitive to the beauty in things, to the meaning in material, even to the life in death — a gambolling grasshopper, a rambling sod-jumper — and seeks to recreate its essence with the materials at hand.

(Often at the expense of material security.) Psychologist and myth monger — and I only mean that in the best way possible — Jordan Peterson suggests the artist teaches us to see things we have forgotten or ignored in our need to simplify the complexity of life.[54] They reawaken the old vision of wonder, for we must become like children to be born again. Artists can be the canaries in our existential coal mine, but in addition to mortal danger, they may also alert us to dangerous beauty, numinous truth, and even intimations of immortal meaning. Peterson's myth-interpretation of Scripture — and I only mean that in the best way possible — is more than a myth-take, for as he himself says, it is only one layer of interpretation and does not exhaust the creative possibilities inherent in the narrative. (Echoing C.G. Jung's "Psychology...is not in a position to make metaphysical statements.")[55]

Indeed, perhaps creativity is simply the word given to describe the willingness to search in the invisibly vast, unlimited wealth of universal potential for a thing waiting to be found. As with King Arthur, there is for each of us a unique vocational sword waiting to be pulled from its exclusively proffering stone.

But who, after all, is an artist? Who is this rare creature? Perhaps, in a manner of speaking, the artist is not so rare. Perhaps every one of us is an artist of sorts, for an artist is one who speaks beauty into life, and life into beauty, even at times against one's own will and fallen nature. We all have a jump of grasshopper in our soul, and plenty of responsible ant as well. Our vocation is a speaking forth, broadcasting our location by occupational echolocation. We are all professionals, for we profess daily our hidden intentions by our actions. For this life is not only a vocation, but an audition. We must hear to speak, and speak to hear.

There are times when we must repopulate our imaginations, for in our maturing efforts to simplify life as a strategy of control and workability, we become blind to the true complexity of this universe. It is never a good idea to turn a blind eye to anything except, perhaps, a blinding light. Indeed, there are times when a bowing of the head is in order, for we cannot mentally encompass the vast plethora of God, whose infinite complexity can appear as undifferentiated simplicity. Our senses cannot encompass that which they cannot detect. We cannot see what we cannot see. We must reduce and narrow the complexity to even function at all. But a pendulum may easily swing too far. Indeed, we know there are colors we cannot see and sounds we cannot hear — why would we think we could know all there is to know of a transcendent God simply for our lack of sense?

So then, just as Isaac Newton named the visible colors hidden in light a "spectrum" — that is, literally a sort of spirit, an apparition hidden in plain sight — let us view God as the Spirit He is, mostly hidden to our senses, but revealed in spirit, whose works we can only observe in a very narrow bandwidth. We know so little. Mystery is the foundation of our fragmentary knowledge. For as Erwin Schrödinger says, "The sensation of color cannot be accounted for by the physicist's objective picture of light-waves."[56] This subjective sensation some call "qualia". We experience most of our existence in this manner. We feel before we think. We experience, then try to make sense of experience. Vocation is a way to ground our emotion and apprehension in a structured mode of application.

I have heard it said one must leave one's comfort zone to grow as an individual. But perhaps this is too univocal, though I am well aware of the need to face unpleasantness in the pursuit of a higher good, to "slay our dragons", as Jordan Peterson might say,[57] and to brave emotional chaos in the search for existential gold, or vice versa. But perhaps one's comfort zone is also telling one something else. Perhaps most Tolkienesque hobbits are winsome and effective hobbits for their very hobbitness. The Bilbos and Frodos are the exceptions that prove the rule. Perhaps a grasshopper — in most cases — should be a grasshopper, and an ant — in most cases — an ant. Indeed, this is what I call the Ant Corrective. For the ant collects what the grasshopper will not, and the grasshopper perceives what the ant cannot. But in being themselves, they can help each other, all at the same time. For we are one Body with many parts, and our value lies in each playing their part, for true creativity is the highest form of play. And for some, the highest form of play is not to play. The Ant Corrective suggests our intrinsic value is the value bequeathed to others, for we contribute best when we deviate least.

There was a time in the misty past of my youthful wanderings upon this earth when I found work as something called a "night auditor". This work took place, as one might expect, at night, behind the front desk — and in the back offices — of a large resort complex separated from the ocean by powdery dunes of white sand and protective barriers of tenacious sea grape. During the daylight hours I plied the open waters on a sailboard, experimented with the arrangement of words on a page, and considered the effects of layering paint and semi-translucent mediums on various substrates. I must have slept at some point as well.

The night audit job consisted of — besides details regarding general resort security and the care of guests — carefully and methodically adding up all the invoicing generated over the course of the day, including that from room charges, laundry facilities, restaurants, bars, beach rentals, and so on. It was also a matter of posting all payments regarding that invoicing. Once every invoice was accounted for and every payment posted, a "trial balance" was run on the computer system to see if the debits and credits balanced out. If there was a discrepancy of any amount, no matter how insignificant, this would need to be found and corrected before morning, for everything from that day needed to balance out to the penny before the paperwork could be sent up to accounting, for how can an accountant account if the bookkeeping is incorrect?

It would be simplistic of me to say there is a Holy Auditor upstairs keeping track of accounts, that there is a trial balance in motion, a sort of spiritual bookkeeping in progress. But then I do love simplicity. So then: on balance, we are all on trial, all will be accounted for, and yet — in Christ — held unaccounted. For our audition is quantified in mega hurts (forgive me), the harm we cause monitored in unrighteous oscillations. Thanks be to God we as Christers are fitted with the Master's noise-cancelling Headphones. For Christ is our Head and we can only have ears to hear if our earways are clear of pandemoniac contamination.

Talk is cheap, and can lead to inner bankruptcy. Silence is golden, for the inaudible cannot be heard without an audition. We must give it space and attention. Indeed, this life is an audition. How well do we play our parts? What are we auditioning for? And what exactly does the word audition mean? Audition literally means "power of hearing or listening". An audition is a test to see how well we hear. How well do we listen? A listening test. And what we need to hear is the message of Christ. This world, this life, is a stage...and a stage. And we — as Shakespeare once said — are merely players.[58] But a Christer is okay with merely playing, for that is our humble approach. We want no more than to play our part, to fulfill our vocation, to pass the audition. For we are each a work of art, an ongoing creative process, whose end is only achieved when no more can be added, and none taken away. That is our completion.

The unity of color is the color of unity. For it is a cohesive tapestry, a body of many parts. And so with vocation. As Mother Theresa is said to have said, "What you are doing, I cannot do, and what I am doing, you cannot do." (I said, "said to have said", for if every quote disattributed to Mother Theresa were a dime — as the saying goes — we would all be swimming in pennies. *Selah*.)

But the point is clear: each must do their part. Vocation is calling; calling frames audition. We say and hear, hear and say. But this is not hearsay. We play our parts freely, and our parts are freely played.

For true beauty is always free, and always leads to great wealth. Ignorance is pricey (not to mention ugly), but beauty — in all its superfluous abundance — is priceless.

Let us contemplate the Grasshopper Criterion, and meditate upon the Ant Corrective. And let us measure the grain of our understanding in like measure. For our shared storehouse is great and our mutual patronage deep.

Pause and consider.

CHAPTER 15

HORSE

<u>PARAFABULON</u>

An old, withered horse told the following tale to a younger horse:

There once was a magnificent stallion.

It was fierce and strong.

It could pull a coach at inestimable speeds hour upon hour, day upon day.

The Coachman loved the stallion, and provided it with only the best food (strictly portioned), shelter (perfectly designed), grooming (performed with minute diligence), and mares (carefully selected).

Yet the Coachman was also stern and demanding.

One day, the stallion said, "Why do you demand such performance?"

The Coachman said, "I see it in you."

The stallion said, "I have been told I would be better on my own, since surely as a horse I would know best my truest path."

The Coachman said, "Do what you will."

And so the stallion — followed by the Coachman's mares and their foals — left the barns and stables and daily provisions and roamed free, ate as much as it could find in the fertile mountains and hills, slept lengthily and profoundly, and frolicked with mares both tame and wild.

Then a day came when a terrible storm loomed upon the horizon. Great winds sprang up. Large hailstones fell from the sky. The horses were terrified, but the stallion said, "Do not be afraid. We will run to the Coachman, for his barns and stables are sturdy, and there we will find shelter."

And so they ran, but when they arrived, the Coachman was gone and every barn and stable was boarded up against the coming storm.

"What will we do?" said the horses.

The stallion said, "We run."

And so they ran and ran, but they could not outrun the storm.

After a long, thoughtful silence, the younger horse said, "Go on."

The old horse gave a start and said, "Excuse me?"

The young horse said, "Oh! Ha — so old. I thought you were sleeping."

The old horse said, "I was."

The young horse said, "The moral of your story is obvious."

"Is it?" said the old horse.

"Of course," said the young horse. "I know this story. We learned it in horse school."

"Did you?" said the old horse.

"Of course," said the young horse. "Better a live horse in captivity, than a dead one in liberty."

"But," said the old horse, "there is more to the story."

"Is there?" said the young horse. "I did not know this."

"Yes," said the old horse. "There is more. For you see, the stallion did not die."

"It did not?" said the young horse.

"No," said the old horse. "It alone survived."

"So...better a live horse in captivity, than...what?" said the young horse.

"What?" said the old horse.

The young horse whinnied in some frustration and said, "What manner of riddle is this? Please, in the end, just tell me the meaning of the parable."

"Who said anything about a parable?" said the old horse. "I

am the stallion."

RUMINATIO

There once was an arrogant and conceited man who owned a horse he could not control. But he was proud of it, for it was large and strong and had a shimmering mane which rippled in the wind. He was the envy of all his neighbors, for they had no such horse. And even though he was constantly injured by this horse — indeed, at times almost to the point of death, for it had very sharp hooves and brilliant nasty teeth and an evil temper — he considered it his most prized possession.

One day, as the mists rose from his fields, he saw another horse which was greater than any he had ever seen or could ever have dreamed of or imagined. It approached him directly, surrounded by a nimbus from the sun, its hooves carving marks into the wet ground which seemed to fill with pools of glimmering gold. All this to say, it appeared to be an extraordinarily nice horse.

The man's other horse, threatened by such a vision of perfection and power — and never one to be controlled or to control itself — instantly attacked the new horse. There was a great battle. It was like a whirlwind to the man, for he felt blinded, and could not discern its constituent elements. But as his vision cleared, he saw the new horse had driven the former into the neighbor's field. The new horse stood firmly planted in the man's field, shining and glorious.

The man tested the new horse mightily, though in the process felt mysteriously tested himself, and found himself not altogether adequate. Nevertheless, his joy was great, for he found the new horse infinitely better than the former horse in every way. He loved the new horse and it seemed the new horse loved him, for not only was it beautiful, but it had saved him from the predatory and unruly behavior of the former. Truly now would he be the envy of all those around.

Later in the evening of that day, the man's neighbor came to his house and asked why the man's former horse was in his field. The man said to the neighbor (much to the neighbor's delight), "Keep it, for I have come into possession of a much greater horse and have not the barn or the field to maintain both."

"Where is this new horse," said the neighbor, "that I might see it?"

"It is in the barn," said the man. "It can be seen tomorrow, for it will be grazing in my field."

The next day, news traveling swiftly, a small crowd gathered at the man's fence to see the new horse. The man proudly brought the amazing creature forth into the field. There was a profound silence from the crowd, which did not surprise the man, for how else would one respond to such transcendence?

But then a thing happened which the man could not understand. The crowd began to laugh, for they could not somehow see the majesty and splendor of the new horse. To them it appeared simply odd, misshapen, and ultimately unremarkable. They left, shaking their heads and patting the neighbor on the back for his amazing good fortune in acquiring the man's former horse.

The man did not know what to think. What enchantment was this? What he saw, no one else could see, and what they saw, he could not see. He sat on a stump, deep in thought, staring in wonder at the beautiful creature before him. What could this mean?

He then reasoned that if the horse acted as it appeared, and appeared as it acted, what else could he do or say but accept it for what it was? And so time went by and the horse showed itself to be everything it ever seemed to promise. The man, without even realizing it, was slowly changed by the irreproachable nature of the horse, for he worked with it daily, not only in his field, but also in the fields of others, for the horse was seemingly inexhaustible, working with consummate goodness and limitless power, and seemed to impart the same spirit unto the man.

And the man was no longer arrogant or boastful in the way of old since he was too busy about his work to care what people thought, even if he had become a laughingstock. However, the neighbors all about the area were amazed at the change which owning and laboring with the new horse had wrought in the man, and were very grateful for the much-needed assistance in their fields. They spoke amongst themselves in wonder.

One said, "Truly he has lost a horse and gained a soul."

And another said, "But wait — he also gained a horse."

And yet another said, "Not much of a horse."

And yet one more said, "Or...so we thought."

For suddenly their eyes were opened.

Pause and consider.

When I was a child, I loved to sit and read in the shade of whatever tree or vine happened to be in the yard of whatever residential structure we happened to be occupying at the time, for it seemed only shade, fiction, and the daily *siesta* could save one from the Bolivian heat. And speaking of riders and horses, I recall reading — as I dodged fire ants and large, horned beetles — a wonderfully illustrated comic strip which I believe is still being published to this day.

In the narrative, Prince Valiant[59] — "Val" to his friends (he smiles a lot) — is a Norwegian prince who makes his way to Camelot and becomes a Knight of the Arthurian Round Table. He has a "Singing Sword" named *Flamberge*, made by the same "person" who fashioned King Arthur's more well-known *Excalibur*. He rides a black horse named Caliburn. (For what is a prince without a trusty steed?) He marries the clever Aleta, Queen of the Misty Isles. He defeats monsters. He (valiantly) fights his way across Europe. He (valiantly) goes to the Holy Land. He (valiantly) even goes to America, (valiantly) visiting

Niagara Falls and socializing with Native Americans (valiantly). He and the clever Aleta spend the entire winter. Their first child is even born in America. This was apparently a thousand years before Columbus.

As I read the captioned text — for there were no word balloons cluttering up the visuals as was the case with my other comics — and marvelled at the detailed and colorful illustrations, my young self pondered the character of this valiant prince, smiling and fighting his way through life. Was he a follower of Christ or was he not? Did it matter? Was this a question I could even ask of a comic? I felt it was, if only because there were constant hints in this direction liberally sprinkled throughout its pages, as indeed there were throughout many of the various comic books neatly shelved against the adobe wall under the corrugated plastic ceiling in my room.

It was very ambiguous, these intimations of Christianity in the Prince, a clear and brilliant cloud which disperses into mist upon closer approach, something I was well familiar with, for at the age of six I recalled finding myself in a small, single-engine airplane with my family, flying over the Andes Mountains towards the Amazon jungle, wherein I was challenged by the pilot to attempt to steer this craft of the air towards a hole in a very solid-looking cloud dead ahead.

I assumed this would be a simple matter, even for a child, but as we winged our way over that distant green broccoli carpet of jungle — in whose apparent sleepy and peaceful depths lay hidden every tropical horror known to personkind — the cloud I was aiming for completely transformed itself into a maze of gauzy mist against the azure sky. I suddenly had no idea where I was, and since clouds now obscured the ground, I could not even discriminate between the vertical and the horizontal. The lesson was clear: one cannot navigate by that which changes at every gust of wind or movement of air. One must navigate by much less temperamental instruments, and by more distant and durable beacons, whose beckoning is sure and whose path is faithful.

So then: it seemed to me that Prince Valiant was a sort of cloud. Indeed, a very beautiful and suggestive cloud, and yet a thing of passing beauty through which one steadily progresses on a journey to a more stable and substantial destination. Therefore, I simply set my literary course to the coordinates of the Master, traveling through the Prince Valiant comics as through any evocative landscape, admiring its many outstanding mythological features and pseudo-Christerical landmarks, baptizing them in the solvent of the Master's discernment, and weaving them into the seamless garment of this one's imagination.

I saw that many narratives were exactly such cloud-like formations, the productions of cultural and historical atmospheric conditions. Indeed, they can be like storm clouds, generating hurricane-force winds of a truly destructive nature, or fresh zephyrs of healing and relief. The temperamental reader may easily be carried away by such turbulent kinetics, but the mature mind in Christ — tethered firmly to the Cornerstone — is unmoved by even the most violent and seductive winds of doctrine, for it is a mind outside of time, calmly judging and discerning in love, constantly sifting earthly chaff to unearth true kernels of heavenly wisdom, revealing and confirming all that is good and right.

For the mind of Christ is an adamantine substance, even as unto the blade of Prince Valiant's *Flamberge*, continually sharpened by the whetstone of opposing dogma. Indeed, the finer the grit of that opposition — the more densely formulated and heavily applied — the keener the blade becomes, engaged at the appropriate angle. (Those who have ears to hear, let them hear.) But this too is learned with experience. In time, it will become invincible, infinitely tensile, unbreakable, for the Master himself did not come to bring peace to the world, but a sword. And the Word of God is active and exceedingly sharp. It penetrates the heart and fillets hidden thoughts, separating decadence and fleshly deceit from the everlasting bones of truth.

But why stop there? It also destroys intellectual strongholds, fanciful arguments, and every arrogant teaching deployed against the knowledge of God.[60] For though any given moment may feel like natural peace, it is in truth supernatural war. However, incarnated as we are, our senses tell us the material world is more primal than the spiritual. But I am talking about metaphysical swords, and a prime cut is meat to our souls.

The cart does not go before the horse. Christ did not come to change the world, but to offer personal salvation...which inevitably changes the world. Such change is a natural byproduct of the sanctified life, for if everyone followed Christ, the world would inevitably change. Christerica is not instrumental; it is personal. But such personal engagement is ultimately instrumental, for in this manner the cart is firmly positioned behind the horse, and progress can subsequently be observed.

Indeed, speaking of carts and horses, I have heard that paired draft horses will take up their customary places without supplementary guidance. They have mastered their positions so well, their positioning no longer requires mastering. Their yoke is then easy and their shared burden light, for they have been willing and well-trained. We also, like unperfected draft horses, have willingly submitted to our training and are gradually Mastering our positions. Indeed, we are rough drafts, but the day will surely come when we will be polished manuscripts, written in the Master's hand, spelling our place perfectly, the Word traced in our training, connecting us in sentences of eternal meaning to the cart of our shared responsibilities.

So then: read the Word, sharpen the mind, and take every thought captive to Christ. Emulate the courage of Prince Valiant riding his trusty steed, embellish upon the canny wisdom of the lovely Aleta, and improvise upon every narrative that is good and true.

Be the *Flamberge* you wish to wield in the world.

And above all, trust the Coachman.

Pause and consider.

CHAPTER 16

RABBIT

PARAFABULON

Two rabbits hopped their way into a noisy village tavern.

They met a third rabbit who had already arrived, arranged for seating, and ordered drinks.

The proprietor was amused to see the three rabbits.

He wished to ask of them questions, but was hard-pressed to keep up with the alimentary responsibilities due his many other regular patrons, who were indeed at that very moment shouting and cursing at him to bring them food and drink, all the while laughing raucously.

The rabbits spoke with one another:

"Had some problems with Weasel. Dug three new openings."

"Two of us chased by Farmer. Both escaped. Cannot catch one if chase two."

"Had race with Turtle. Lost. Again. Cannot seem to focus."

"Afraid of everything. Decided to jump in pond. End it all.

Terrified the frogs. Reality check. Pulled self together."

"Magician keeps dragging me out of hat. Ears hurt. Hat smells."

"More kids."

"Same."

"Gave burrow to neighbor. Bad move. Took over whole warren."

"Same."

"Dog caught me. Bit me. Licked me. Confused. Terrified. Escaped."

"Same."

"Nibbled. Grass. Hay. Nibbled some more."

"Same."

"Carrots."

"Nibbled carrots?"

"Carrots."

"Lucky."

After some time, the two rabbits departed. The third remained, finishing one last drink at the bar.

The proprietor, having overheard some of their conversation, and momentarily experiencing a lull in his ongoing, customer-based abuse, came over to the rabbit.

"How are things at home?" said he.

"Relentless danger and overcrowding; cannot turn without bumping; warrens cramped and tight; young rabbits born and growing everywhere; Weasel and Dog constant danger; forever digging new holes, tunnels; immediately occupied by neighbors; life unfair; overwhelmed," said the rabbit.

"Why then do you come to a rowdy, crowded place like this?" said the proprietor.

"Nobody wants to be alone," said the rabbit.

RUMINATIO

In speaking of rabbits, it would seem unwise of me to turn a blind eye to turtles. For many are familiar with Aesop's fable regarding the tortoise and the hare, in which the turtle wins the race by steadfastly pursuing the course, while the rabbit — though built for speed — loses out in the end due to many distractions along the way. After all, slow and steady does occasionally win the race, and a narrow road, though moderately constricting, may carry one to the sought-after destination more surely and securely (think wetsuit; think knight's armour) than a wide open highway leading towards a cliff. After all, wide is the road that leads to destruction, and welcoming are the devil's rest stops.

Every Christer is — in a sense — a turtle type, running a race we seemingly have no chance of winning, though destined (predestined?) to triumph every time. But many who claim to follow Christ conduct themselves in the manner of a hare, sprinting in all directions to little — or often damaging — consequence. For it is highly intoxicating and more entertaining to dash about with apparent lightness and ease than it is to plod boringly along the same old narrow path. The manna of the Master's truth, though nutritionally complete and abundantly obtainable through Scripture, does not offer the variety and interest many desire, for many quickly tire of God's sufficient provisions, yearning instead for the culture's insufficient perversions, though they be of little use and even less help. Many have replaced the careful and deliberate mining of solid Biblical exegisis with the weedy planting of questionable eisegesis and the self-obsessed consumption of narcigesis. Many have also replaced the limitless well of Sola Scriptura with the shallow puddle of Sola Experientia and the snaring riptides of Sola Cultura.

However, the same old narrow path is not boring to the turtle, and neither should it be to the Christer, for Christurtles are to the manna born. With our nose to the ground, every little thing along our humble way is significant and holy. Our attention is made manifest in our disposition, for our disposition is manifestly attentive.

But the hare cannot stand such a deliberate and steadfast vision, for it sees color and adventure on every side. It must explore every alternate route, every interesting bush, every darkly welcoming tunnel, every distant mountain. It temporarily forgets — or chooses to disregard — the one and only path leading to the one and only destination. As an example, some have recently hopped upon the banal bandwagon of "de-wrathing" God — perhaps better instead to de-rabbit Christerica. For such hares may get lost in warrens of their own making, as indeed their deed-consequence theories predict. Therefore such hares must turtle back, reclaiming tortoisal single-mindedness, despite all temptation to the contrary, for all know they will otherwise lose the race. After all, the stories have spoken.

And yet I do not wish to over-turtle Christerica either, for it is possible for a turtle to withdraw into its shell at the slightest sign of danger, restricting its vision considerably in the process. Often this proves to be an effective temporary survival strategy, but it is not without its own peril, for depending too heavily upon a carapace presupposes an inflexible plastron, and if one is sandwiched immovably between both, how is it possible to maneuver correctively or creatively? What does this even mean? It is possible I do not know. However, I may have some ideas.

One of the many homes we temporarily occupied when I was a child — in Cochabamba, City of Eternal Spring — had a walled garden in the back yard. I say yard, but in reality it was a sort of dense and complicated ecosystem which I believe to this day has never been fully mapped or catalogued. (After all, why would it be? It was only a yard. However, perhaps there are discoveries to be made even in — or especially in — one's own back yard.)

There were areas in that tangled labyrinth even an inquisitive child like myself never fully penetrated. It was too deeply complex, especially for one more interested at the moment in tossing lighted firecrackers at opposing boyhood factions, and escaping discipline for the resulting hole blown out of the jacket. Nevertheless, in the yard there was complicated flora. And undocumented fauna. (As previously mentioned.) There was even an actual human family who lived mysteriously beyond the border of the back wall yet gained access through our property from the dusty street out front, entering via the front gate, skirting the front yard, traveling along the shaded breezeway at the side of the house (past our two uninterested dogs sheltering from the heat), and finally making their way through the uncharted complexity of the back yard. I have still not — to this day — completely understood this arrangement, but at the time it seemed like nothing out of the ordinary.

However, there was a very large turtle living in that prodigal enclosure. And if space and time are supposedly a continuum, no scientist ever confirmed this in our yard, for in examining this turtle, such a scientist would have discovered that though it occupied a measurable space, its time component was at great variance with ours, for it would remain motionless for days and weeks, then suddenly alter its location, which from our perspective seemed to occur in an instant, yet from the turtle's perspective must have taken a substantial length of time. All we could do was throw bananas in its perceived direction in hopes the turtle would find nourishment therewith.

In this manner night and day continued their eternal somersaulting, and the weeks — for us in any case — flowed past. Until one day, out of random curiosity — and perhaps some concern — we came to wonder where indeed the turtle might be at that very moment on our space and time, for we had not caught sight of it for some while. It was not easy to find, but it was indeed finally found. The poor turtle — there is no way to put this delicately (trigger warning) — was dead. It had become lodged (terrapinned, so to speak) between some man-made structure on one side and some firmly planted vegetation on the other, both immovable and both now lost to my descriptive memory. But in any case, a space too constricting for the large turtle to move forward, backward, or to the side. And so it starved.

And so — I thought to myself at the time — that can happen. I paused and I considered. It reminded me of a stalemate in chess. One can live life in such a manner that there are no moves left. And looking around — or even ahead — is not a simple thing when sheltering inside an impenetrable shell of pride, ignorance, or anything else. And yet, gluttony is not the answer to starvation; junk food is not the answer to hunger; heresy is not the answer to confusion and doubt. Proper spiritual fitness rests upon a steady regime of both faith and works, featuring a balanced "nous"-tritional diet of Scripture and the practice of Godly virtues. (That is, "nous", as in the sense of the Greek "intellect".)

But I am speaking of rabbits, all evidence to the contrary, for it seems these testudinal tangents are convicting me of my own form of distracted coneyism. In self-justification I will say that rabbits are not all bad, even as metaphors, for they are symbolic of new life and the social conviviality which is a hallmark of what it means to be a human being. My harp — as is evident by this point in this book — has been tuned to the refrain of "crowd-as-untruth", but what of the sweet melody of community? Rabbits avoid solitude. Sometimes at all cost. But to avoid solitude may cost all, for it is only one's solitary moments which give meaning to community.

So then: what of community? We acknowledge the seeker may often find company in silence, and silence in company, for it is far easier to lose oneself in a crowd than in the forest. That is to say, community is subjective. One person's crowd is another's community, and one person's community another's crowd. And according to the Master, where even two or three are gathered in his name, there will he be also.[61] We cannot be with everybody all the time. Or even some of the time. We trust the Master to guide us into the sort of community most suitable to our unique, individual natures. And that, of course, may differ from person to person.

If, for instance, one with a gift of solitude finds a mode of community in the company of so-called dead authors, if the so-called dead authors are in Christ, are they not spiritually alive even now? And if that collective in turn sharpens one as iron upon iron as the Master sees fit, is this not community? For all those alive in Christ — even now — are also dead in

Christ, and those dead in Christ are even now alive. Thus one justifies one's book-lined study. Thus one justifies literature, for it is truly a vast assembly of witnesses.

Indeed, perhaps great literature is not an escape from reality, as some might suggest, but a plunge beneath its waves. For what we call reality is only a surface impression whose depths remain uncharted without the narrative vessel required to explore its manifold dimensions. To say great fiction is an escape from reality is like saying travel by submarine is an escape from the ocean. In truth, if it is an escape, it is only an escape from the surface, for the submarine, like the technology of the storifying human mind itself, is the device most capable of exploring the vast substructures of reality. Great fiction is exploratory, and may even generate its own oceans. But these oceans may be exactly what is required for the sort of spiritual travel God has in mind. And if there be fellow travelers upon these narrative oceans who no longer make formal appearance in one's current dimension, this is not to say they are unconditionally constrained by their alleged absence. However, one need not altogether refrain from fraternizing with fellow spirits currently enfleshed.

But who requires such communitarian advice? Not many, for if one is reading this, one is human, and therefore social. Still, even in a group, one can feel lonely, even lost. For our sacred discontent is manifest not only in the Christer continually deconstructing cultural forms and generating new modes of thought (paraphrasing Herbert Schneidau),[62] but also in a form of nostalgia and homesickness that no home can ever fully satisfy. And nostalgia is no joke. People once died of it quite frequently (when it was considered a medical condition), and most likely still do, even though its symptoms have now been defined away into various other health disciplines. We all know this nameless feeling, this strange wistfulness, this unhoused homesickness. It is sometimes even called the blues, and displayed for public show upon the strings of a steel guitar, sliding up and down upon its scales of hope and regret. For we are all yearning for the innocence we have lost; for the rich, mellifluous communal safe harbor of God and Garden.

C.S. Lewis felt he had discovered an inkling of proof for the existence of God in the feeling described by the German word *Sehnsucht*. This sensation, argued Lewis, would only be possible if there existed some reality to satisfy it in a similar manner to actual food existing to satisfy the ache of physical hunger. For *Sehnsucht* describes a permanent sense of sweet, inconsolable longing, a yearning for "that unnameable something, desire for which pierces us like a rapier at the smell of a bonfire, the sound of wild ducks flying overhead, the title of *The Well at the World's End*, the opening lines of *Kubla Khan*, the morning cobwebs in late summer, or the noise of falling waves."[63]

Now, I have to admit, the sound of wild ducks flying overhead does not evoke in me quite the same response. I myself might simply duck (so to speak); another might even reach for a shotgun. And the smell of a bonfire? Not so desirable when fuelled by pressure-treated lumber. (Though no less rapier-like for all that.) But what of the opening lines of Kubla Khan?

In Xanadu did Kubla Khan
A stately pleasure-dome decree:
Where Alph, the sacred river ran
Through caverns measureless to man
Down to a sunless sea.[64]

Well, enough to say C.S. Lewis was a romantic. Clearly. One understands and sympathizes. But as expressive as Coleridge's words may be, they do not generate within me quite the same fever of nostalgia as in Lewis. And neither, perhaps, in Coleridge himself, for he is quoted as saying, "I never had the essentials of poetic Genius, but merely mistook a strong desire for original power." And, "Like the ostrich, I cannot fly, yet have wings that give me the feeling of flight." Which is a very poetic manner in which to decry one's lack of poetic genius. However, I do myself experience a slight prickle of adrenaline at the sound of falling waves, and even occasionally a powerful thirst. One person's *Sehnsucht* (longing) may be another's *Verlangen* (desire). However, thank God living water is abundantly available.

Bolivia shares a border with Brazil, but very little else. No two peoples could be more unalike, for I have traveled from Bolivia to Brazil (and back again) via the Death Train out of Santa Cruz, and so have seen everything — yes, anthropologically and zoologically, but also existentially — for not only did I experience transcendent whirlwinds of yellow butterflies as I journeyed towards resplendent waterfalls, but also the typhoid-visaged stare of death on a sickbed.

But I wish to speak of nostalgia, and that is indeed something these two peoples share, as we all do. (As I did as I convalesced, ate warm pudding, and for some bewildering reason spun Fleetwood Mac's *Rumours* album over and over upon our record turntable. Was it the only music we had? Why? I have no idea.) The Brazilians — a deeply emotional, sensitive, and sensual people — have a word *"saudade"* which is the ultimately untranslatable expression of this thing under consideration. Indeed, they celebrate it with a national holiday, the *"Dia da Saudade"*. January 30. (And then comes Carnival, the most outrageous, manic, bacchanalian festival one can possibly imagine. And then Easter. One may well ponder the meaning and function of this calendrical segment of the uniquely Brazilian cultural liturgy on one's own time.)

Truly, *saudade*, nostalgia, homesickness, *sehnsucht*, the blues, whatever hue of loss and longing one imagines, they are all just shades of melancholy. And expounding upon melancholy, well, there are few pleasures in life more satisfying than sitting in a well-worn leather armchair by a (smokeless) roaring fire, putting one's feet up, accessing a flavourful mug of hot chocolate — now I am getting nostalgic, never mind the flying ducks — and reading from Robert Burton's *Anatomy of Melancholy*. For there is no more encyclopedic treatment of melancholy to be found on the face of the earth. In its one-thousand-plus-pages of densely packed prose, one can view melancholy — and much else — from every possible angle.

But it would be a mistake to suppose this is depressing or pedantic. In fact, it is a delightful book, a compendium of laugh-out-loud excoriation, a prism of righteous ridicule, full of wisdom, nonsense, and superannuated knowledge, home to an innumerable host of rousing insults and razor-sharp rants. Really, one of the best books ever.

But Robert Burton's "rhapsody of rags gathered together from several dunghills" is a rabbit hole which I will repent of the temptation to warren at this time. As suggested earlier, I must turtle back. However...however, to the immediate point, since we are indeed upon this path, does the comprehensive Burton reference turtles at all? Indeed, yes. He mentions the inhabitants of England "are *testudines testa sua inclusi*, like so many tortoises in our shells, safely defended by an angry sea, as a wall on all sides". Fair enough. But to us an angry sea is little protection against ballistic projectiles, for ascendant demons angrily see our gain as their loss, and a watery shell no barrier to our Adversary, the prince of the power of the air. Our shell is Christ, for with Christ as our shell, the Adversary-launched shells cannot win against the shell game of our salvation, for the Master's sleight of hand crucifies such soaring attacks, nailing the enemy with our humble shuffling. The angle of attack is too unpretentiously low for the Adversary's prideful high.

So then: a turtle, knowing its limits, limits its knowing. Its groove is low, and modestly does it sow. The trusty turtle does not cultivate its existential planting with unnecessary knowledge, neither does it hide forever in its shell, nor is it harebrained, for this would be physically impossible based upon its biological constraints. But a hare, striving for thoughtful patience and thought-filled self-restraint, may yet turtle back, center down, and deliberate. Indeed, such intentional deliberation can lead to more meaningful liberation. And in such manner, the tortoise and the hare may journey together, in fellowship, reaching their desired destination as one, the turtled hare gracing herr turtle's unhurried, unharried pace.

For I have learned if a shooter chases two rabbits in a field, he will catch none.

And if a shooter chases one rabbit in a garden, the garden will be destroyed.

But if a shooter chases a rabbit in a bar, the rabbit will be lost. For a rabbit chasing mixed spirits may be unaware of the shot. (Those who have twitching ears, let them hear.)

So then: turtle back, my hare-y friends, turtle back. Get low. (Even lower.)

Quaff if you must an exorcised mocktail from the intellectual bar of life, and slowly — yes, oh, so lowly — lowtail it home.

Pause and consider.

CHAPTER 17

SPIDER

PARAFABULON

In a castle high above a village there labored a maidservant and a cook.

"Of drudgery there seems no limit," said the maidservant. "Hours I spend daily in every endless room — and every nook and cranny — endlessly dusting and sweeping cobwebs."

The cook said, "It is a marvel insignificant creatures such as spiders lay claim to a life within the king's castle."

"Marvel not," said the maidservant, "for their webbing is my energy ebbing, their tangle my nerves a-jangle."

The cook said, "No spiders, no webs."

The maidservant said to herself, "Right is the cook. If but rid the castle of spiders I am able, no longer will webs remain, and sweetness and light my work will be."

So saying, she used many ancient means and remedies to trap and kill the spiders that occupied the king's castle.

A day finally came where she saw not one web throughout all

the rooms. All the spiders were gone.

And she was very happy, for it seemed her yoke would be easy and her burden light.

But the next day the cook came running and said, "The castle is full of flies!"

The king summoned the maidservant and said, "What has happened? Why have flies entered the castle in such droves?"

"Sir, alas," said the maidservant, "no spiders are there to in their webs catch...them."

"Is there no other solution?" said the king. "Speak or lose your head."

"Screens," said the maidservant, off the top of her head.

"Screens?" said the king. "What manner of beast be these?"

"Beasts are they not," said the maidservant, "a type of webbing they be, by man built to over every open window place. No longer to enter will the flies be able and required no longer will the spiders either be."

"Install them immediately!" said the king.

And everything was fine except, of course, there were now screens on every window.

The king did not like this, for the purpose of windows was to him unobstructed views.

"Remove the screens!" said the king.

"My liege, but," said the maidservant, "once again will flies return, then to capture them spiders, then dusting and sweeping of cobwebs many daily hours required. Of me."

"Here is a thought," said the king. "Why not just do your job?"

RUMINATIO

Gabriel García Márquez — author of the magical realist novel *One Hundred Years of Solitude* — once said his fellow South Americans were all creatures of an unbridled reality whose crucial problem was the lack of conventional means to render their lives believable.[65] And I believe it, for my childhood travels and travails throughout Bolivia's mountain-clad psychography — jungle on one side, inaccessible sea (perpetually soon to be reclaimed) on the other — would take many unconventional manuscripts to depict. Indeed, I am writing them even now, though webbed in fiction and netted with myth, for I too am spinning the means of rendering my life believable, as it has been largely surreal up to this point.

In my experience, Bolivian spiders were certainly of the unbridled variety, though easily rendered believable by the conventional means of loudly screaming, pointing, and fleeing. Now, I am neither an arachnophobe, nor am I pro-arachnid. So long as they do their thing — outside, in the wild, where they belong — I will do them no harm. If, though, they are to be encountered within the realm of my living space, one of us must go. And it will not be me if I have anything to say about it. For my home is not the overlapping intersection of a Venn diagram illustrating our individual ecosystems. The spider must wend its own way and I mine. We represent non-overlapping magisteria, though mine is portable and deployed as a sphere of spider-resistant personal space ranging to several feet around me in all directions no matter where I travel. (I suppose it is the same for the spider, simply in reverse. Must our magisteria battle forever?)

I would not want anyone to think, though, that I am not impressed by the ability of the spider. For many are the times I have watched — outside, in nature, well beyond my sphere of personal space — a spider lightly abseiling through the air by a line of self-extruded silk, its anchor some distant potential, its destination known only to the wind, the perfect picture of faith on the line. But that faith is almost always warranted, for faith travels well, and with patience often will achieve its purpose.

From there it is a matter of awe to watch a spider do its job and spin its web. What manner of engineering be this? Where is such delicate yet supple rendering learned? Where the instruction in such useful geometry? (These questions, of course, are simply rhetorical. One must answer them as one sees fit. And survival will go to the fittest.)

The spider's web is a thing of incredible sensitivity. The

smallest tremor generated by whatever source is immediately transmitted to the spider. Most times it can identify its prey simply by the amplitude of that vibration. From then on the details are too gruesome to consider, but I do wonder what a spider makes of my facial features inadvertently activating — and shredding — its carefully structured net. For my part, I do not care for the mesh of another's magisteria draped over my face — indeed, I cannot countenance it — and work swiftly to remove it.

However, not all spiders have webs. When my parents visited fellow workers in the deep Bolivian jungle — and we children along with them, as prisoners led to the gallows — we were told to always check our shoes for tarantulas before installing them upon our feet. I remember thinking two things: if I ensconced my foot against a tarantula in my shoe, I would die. If I checked my shoe first, and there was a tarantula in it, I would also die. So I was going to die either way. Best to leave shoes out of it altogether. This is when I began to realize the wisdom — as the locals obviously did — of going barefoot at all times, for to protect oneself is only useful if one is actually protecting oneself. After all, armor is only armor if it functions as armor. Otherwise it is dead weight, a terminal overcoat, a killing casket of conservation, a receptacle of expiration.

Indeed, perhaps there are times when it is better — as with the web of the spider — to be highly sensitive to the nature of one's interactions with the environment, for a delicate lattice of grace may be a vastly more powerful existential deployment than an impenetrable wall of ideology. For every human organization is inherently corrupt, even those founded — and populated — by so-called Christians, for a Christian does not a Christer make. Indeed, every human organization mysteriously takes on a life of its own whose primary concern — as with most organisms — is its own survival. Individuals are always demoted to functionaries in the service of such organizations.

But this is the beauty of Christerica. It is a body of individuals. One might say this too is structure, and one would be right. But it is not built by human hands or minds. It is superorganic, not suborganizational. It is a spiritual reality cohering in irrational obscurity whose individual components are still radically individual in human terms, and who are knitted together into a web of being one can only begin to apprehend by faith. For our spirits are like filaments in the light fixtures of our bodies. We light up as the Master's energy flows through us. We must function as nodes of goodness in the web of grace — sleek, supple, smooth, (*geschmeidig*, in the German) but permanently interconnected, a numinous neural network, a Lordly limbic system.

Many will find this perfectly natural to consider, for many interact constantly via the internet, the worldwide web, and so on. And though much of this takes place in a metaphorical cloud, I have it on good authority that it is dependent upon electrons flowing through circuits cleverly arranged within — and information operating between — various devices. The flow in the weblike, netlike circuits is regulated in some respect — again, good authority — by objects called resistors, transistors, and capacitors. Each has their crucial function in the circuit, as does the Christer in the matrix of the Spirit. So let us resist where we must, maximize our output from our input, and wisely modify — as led — the ratio of self capacitance to mutual capacitance.

And let us not only be electronically metaphorical, but let us also use our minds and spirits to screen, sieve, and filter in real terms. For the Mishnaic *Pirkei Avot* speaks of four types of learners: the sponge, the funnel, the strainer, and the sieve. The sponge indiscriminately soaks everything up. The funnel absorbs nothing, for everything runs through. The strainer retains the dregs but loses the wine. But the sieve — the sieve filters out the chaff of worldly foolishness, leaving only the finest flour of wisdom and knowledge.

Christopher Alexander, in his book *The Luminous Ground*, speaks of reality as an elegant fretwork of centers, an embedded "I"-ness in all things, immanent in nature. But why and how? He reasons only something like the concept of God produces such things. But this troubles him for he can find nothing to occupy that concept, for who believes in a personal God anymore? The answer, of course, is obvious — I do. As do many others. For the Christer believes there is a God, active and personal, whose "I"-ness is not shy-ness, and whose "my"-ness is not why-ness. For even Job did not receive the answers he sought, but rather the "I"-ness God brought.

So then: every thing is its own center, but is it centered? For there are many centers, but Christ is our center, for one does not live by bread alone, especially if one is gluten-free. There is no "center" to the universe, for the universe is its own center. The sun is the center of its universe. The earth is the center of its universe. I am the center of my universe. My cat is the center of its universe. And so on. And yet at the center of our own being is an existential vacuum; we are empty, for our center is the center of its universe, which is nothingness. Indeed, our centers are filled with all that we perceive.

Some centers, though, are more constrained than others. Some have a quite radical freedom of movement. Some have the ability to move and arrange other centers. And some have the faith to transfer their self-centeredness to the one true center of existence, which is Christ. It's a sort of spiritual banking: one can either precariously hoard one's value, or one can deposit that value securely in Christ. One's value then only exists by proxy, yet there is a guaranteed eternal return.

As an aside, slightly off center, free will and the appearance of free will are functionally indistinguishable from each other at the higher levels from any perspective but the omniscient. One could say that at the level where the constraints are not fully apparent to the center in question, they cease to be determining factors in any practical or measurable sense for that center. Only a higher center would have the capability to observe the constraints. Therefore in reality there is no paradox between God's sovereignty and human free will. There are simply levels of awareness regarding contingency.

In one sense, God alone in all of existence is the only being without free will since in His omniscience He is aware of all possible constraint. He will always act in accordance with His infinite lack of constraint. He says it Himself: "I am that I am." He is what He is. He can be no other. He will always act in accordance with His nature. He is the one thing in all existence that will never change. He is the unchanging, the unmovable center. He is not a contingent being. Or rather, He is contingent only upon His noncontingent Self.

In another sense, then, God is the only being radically free of determinacy, for He alone has no pre-existent cause. He is not an effect. He is both cause and effect, though neither. He is affect. As the old saying goes, "Precause He lives, I can grace tomorrow."

But we, being contingent beings, are in some sense a Christerical representation of the multifaceted jewels populating the Buddhist concept of Indra's Net. I say in some sense, but not every sense, for though we are indeed nodes in a transcendent tapestry, we are not only reflections of each other, ad infinitum, but of Christ (ad infinitum). So not exactly an Indranet, but an Infranet, a Christernet, lets say, top-down in architecture, but bottom-up in its earthy resurrection modality. There is a distinctly Christlike pattern to our design. We are a transcendent area rug whose dimensions are measured by the incarnational intentions of Christ's will, for he is the Weaver and we are the woven. His is the warp and his is the weft. And we as Christers are the warping and wefting in the numinous fabric of the Master's artistry.

I have read that in quantum mechanics — for everything seems to have gone quantum these days, even mechanics — elementary particles exhibit a property called "spin". There is some indeterminacy in regards to this spin which is suggestive at a subatomic level of the nature of free will. Or not. Indeterminacy — depending upon one's viewpoint — is either underdetermined or overdetermined, for we know — or think we know — that every unknown is a degree of freedom, but, as Donald Rumsfeld once said, "There are known knowns. These are things we know that we know. There are known unknowns. That is to say, there are things that we know we don't know. But there are also unknown unknowns. There are things we don't know we don't know."

Therefore, we definitely know we do not know the things we do not know. And the things we do not know we do not know may be exactly the things which matter most. For all matter matters matter. Indeed, all matter is a matter of mattering. Otherwise who would care? Matter matters because it is matter. But it is precisely matter because it matters. All is connected and interconnected. The fabric of spacetime is not only a net, but a blanket. For how else would we dream these dreams without this web of wonder to warm and enfold us? Indeed, subatomic spin is eiderdown or up. (Forgive me.)

We — like a web — are spun, though we spin not. But if we spin, we spin up, for we are Homespun, God's *geschmeidig* gossamer.

We screen as we are screened. We project as we are

projected.

For a screen of the appropriate gauge will capture the projected image.

And the net image is Christ, if in his living web we are truly caught.

Pause and consider.

CHAPTER 18

PIG

PARAFABULON

"It is not like we invited him."

"Why would he sleep in our mud?"

"Makes no sense. Totally prodigal."

"Humans are unbelievable. So smart, yet so stupid."

"He has a home. Why not go back there?"

"Independence! I want my independence! Give me my inheritance now!"

"Hard to even look at him. So stupid."

"What do we do?"

"Leave him alone. Guaranteed he will not stay forever."

"But in the meantime?"

"Root around him."

"If it were me, and I were the father, I would not take him

back."

"I feel much the same. But then we are only hogs and if-"

"Wait — is he…?"

"He is; he is eating our feed!"

"That is uncalled for."

"We do our best; we do everything by the book; now this."

"It gets a little depressing."

"Thanks for nothing, life."

"No kidding."

"You know what I like, though?"

"What is it?"

"He does not think he is too good for us."

"That is surely clear."

"When has that ever happened?"

"Probably never."

"Like, in history?"

"Maybe."

"He is friendly enough."

"I guess."

"I feel like he has brought us a little higher."

"How?"

"Like, we are a bit on his level because he has come down to our level."

"Right."

"He is our superior, but look at him, eating and grovelling there."

"I know what you are saying."

"If he went, would you go with him?"

"Where?"

"I do not know. Where he goes. If he goes."

"I might."

"Probably."

"If he let me."

"Would he eat us?"

"What?"

"You know, eat. Us."

"No. More of a chance we would eat him, actually. His kind, they do not eat us."

"Is that true?"

"That is true."

"Why?"

"They only eat those that chew cud and have split hooves."

"But we do have split hooves."

"But we do not chew cud."

"So?"

"I do not know. Somehow it makes us unclean."

"Better unclean and uneaten, than clean and eaten, I always say."

"When? When have you said this?"

"Okay, never. But we are safer with him if he goes than if we stay in this pen?"

"We are safer with him."

"Well, let us go then."

"He is not going yet. He only sits and thinks."

"But when he does — if he does — we go with him."

"Okay. Yes. We go wherever he goes and stay wherever he stays."

"A simple plan."

"Dead simple."

"Wait, what? Dead?"

"I take it back."

"Much better."

"Stay close to him. Do not let him out of your sight."

"Not a chance. We are going home, for his home is our home."

"Best day of my life."

R U M I N A T I O

Pigs are not unintelligent. In truth, I have heard exactly the opposite, and I have no reason to doubt such hypothecation, for I have seen much to marvel at in this life, even regarding swine, though personal experience has been limited to bacon, ham, and pork chops. And sausage. This, I suppose, is their revenge, for such food can be deadly to the body, however good it may seem to the mouth. Indeed, if it can be said that eyes are gateway to the soul, then surely it can be said with even more confidence that the mouth is gateway to the belly, and teeth that gateway's undependable guardians.

I say undependable guardians for a reason, and that reason is I have a bone to pick with teeth. This toothpick, so to speak, is a bone of contention whose sharp point probes beyond the gum line of common denticulation into the darker realms of evil lurking near the anchoring roots, for there is no surer sign of evil in the world than teeth. Consider only their inexorably devilish decay, miserable mesial drift, and potential (often realized) for mortal pain, and one will easily find sufficient confirmation of what I call — in my private philosophical moments — the Dental Proof. For our common inheritance of such toothy fallibility is definitive confirmation of a sinful nature. We know this; we experience this; we combat this. For what else is a toothbrush but a weapon of war wielded in the battle for oral hygiene? We struggle daily — if responsive to the not-always-persuasive recommendations of trained professionals — to limit the immoral influence of external particles upon the flawed inner temple of our toothy henge. For the word oral becomes moral with a simple compression of defensive lips, and odontology is to ontology as biting is to being.

So then: teeth are unambiguous evidence of our personal defilement, our existential affliction. But teeth are not the enemy. They are simply the most visible lightning rod of entropy. Poor teeth — I almost feel sorry for them. But then I feel even more sorry for myself. And I will not even begin to speak of periodontal disease, for like a sow after washing, why return to wallow in the mud of one's own misery?

As one looks back upon one's life — and indeed, forward as well — it seems the grinding subtext of one's entire life could be simply a battle with, against, and for one's teeth. Thanks be to God current dentistry has advanced to a reasonable state of effectiveness and painlessness, for as a child it was the portal to a realm of nightmare, a metallic foretaste of the very gates of clinical hell. There never will be words sufficient to describe the childhood terror and horror of early Bolivian dentistry. Never have I questioned more earnestly the justification for my existence than when sitting on the cold leather chairs in the waiting room of that dentist's office off Cochabamba's busy *El Prado* boulevard.

The outrageous contingency of human existence first exerted its full existential force upon my young self in that waiting room. Outside: the weather was beautiful, the sun was shining, the palm trees were...palming, birds were flitting, people were walking gaily, talking animatedly, and laughing joyously. Inside: cold, clinical terror reigned; also fear and trembling. How could this be? Just ten feet away — at most — life was beautiful. Why, I thought, must I endure this? Surely I could escape. There was no lock on the door, no security guard, no inclement weather. (C.S. Lewis, my Narnian friend, says the gates of hell are locked from the inside. How true!)[66] But where was I to run? The evil was in my own mouth. I would only carry it with me. So I sat and endured horror by the mouthful, praying for some unarticulated mouthy miracle which never arrived. Nor did I truly expect it, for nothing short of the Advent of Christ and the end of all worlds would suffice. And surely my insignificant pain — though a world of misery to my young self — was not sufficient cause for the breaking in of the Parousia.

No, when it came to dentistry, I was on my own. There was no so-called safe space for me to retreat into, for my defilement was intrinsic, and the only means of momentary redemption was to move forward into the dentist's toothy Holy of Holeys, replete with drills, needles, and any number of assaultive stainless steel artifacts arrayed on the altar of a steel tray. I was triggered, sure enough, but wished I had been shot.

I soon learned that when it came to teeth, my alternatives were either ongoing pain and discomfort accompanied by long-term decay, or greater momentary pain — notice the word "greater" and tremble, for this was no joke — accompanied by a measure of subsequent relief and longer-term decay. In either case — my mind telescoping along the hallways of time — death was the obvious final destination and outcome. There was no getting off this ride of life, a truth removing the bulk of amusement from the potential enjoyment of the days ahead. For as the sages have said, as long as one has teeth, one is guaranteed pain. Life, after all, is suffering.

Perhaps this was when I had my first experience with death salience, for there are moments when abstract notions become concrete and fantasy gives way to reality. The Dental Proof is incontrovertible. Tooth decay is a replicating signpost on the road to the grave. Every childhood appointment with the dentist was symbolic of life's final appointment with death. After one such harrowing appointment, I simply sat on a bench facing the roundabout preceding the bridge over the *Rio Rocha*, closed my eyes, and let the warmth of the tropical Andean sun pervade my body, knowing full well these very perceptions would one day cease and I would no longer roam this earth or occupy the dentist's chair. For every one of us is a window of perception upon this world, briefly opening and closing as time allows. As such, we vary one to another in regards to individual clarity and coverage of the landscape. Some are expansive picture windows; others only peepholes. Our individual personalities, faith perceptions, and protean wills determine the meaningful dimensions of each unique univocal viewscape.

In that moment of early death salience, I experienced a strangely calm acceptance of the fact. But perhaps I was only in shock, for such moments are more often accompanied by panic than resignation.

However, this particular salience is not salient to the moment, for I wish to sink my remaining teeth into more satisfying subject matter. That is, into the metaphorical meat of literary hoggery and political pigskinnery. After all, who cares about dying when there is living to be done? Dying is easy. Living is hard. It takes some effort. And even a little faith.

Stories featuring swine often seem to be heavily flavored with political symbolism. Perhaps this is because pigs are very social, and the social nearly always leads to the political. Communal nesting, hierarchies of dominance, and highly developed vocal communication validate hogs for allegorical application. The Scriptures themselves condemn pigs as unclean, perhaps even a symbol — along with dogs — for gentile unbelievers. Why is chewing the cud a prerequisite for animal cleanliness? We do not know, though we suspect the diet required by such an animal does not defile it. Cud-chewers will not be eating rotting corpses or the like. But pigs might. A few years ago a story appeared of a man who was eaten by his own hogs.[67] The only remaining evidence found in the enclosure were a few pieces of his body and his dentures. I cannot stop thinking about those dentures. That detail. Especially considering the death salience of the Dental Proof mentioned above. It is uncanny, these thoughts of the perishable and imperishable.

"Do not cast pearls before swine," says the Master, for value has no value to those with no understanding of value. And so with the Christer. Let us be wise with our pearls. Discernment is the fruit of wisdom, and dentures the antithesis of decay. Be not like the Biblical Gadarenes who pleaded with the Master to leave after he had cast out demons from two possessed men and into a large herd of pigs who then rushed over a steep bank into a lake and died in the water.[68] The pearl of great price was before them, yet they were more concerned about hogs and temporal well-being. But well-being is not being well, for being well is to be well-born. And the Christer is a well-born, teething piglet searching for the hand casting the pearl, for to be cast in the caster's hand is to be cast well and to be well-castable. There is therefore no castigation to them which are in Christ Jesus,[69] who cast not after the flesh, but after the Spirit. *Selah.*

In the novel, *Charlotte's Web*, author E.B. White has Charlotte the spider attempting to save Wilbur the pig from being slaughtered. Her strategy: spinning his words into her web which the humans mistakenly read as evidence of the divine. It is a bittersweet story, for — spoiler alert — Charlotte dies, though Wilbur survives. I only introduce this tale for one principal reason: it features a pig. My point being, I suppose, in the same way this author created a pig-related story, God also created His own pig-related story, and we are in it. Why create pigs to simply forbid their consumption, cast demons into, and warn of casting pearls before? Perhaps that is exactly why. Never underestimate a creator, for a creator's intentions may not always be obviously apparent from the creator's inventions.

So then: to a swine like Wilbur, casting a pearl before it may possibly have some worth, for it is yet possible for a pig to be pearlworthy, given its creator's interventions and its own intentions. Sacrifice is a pearl whose rejection is always piggish, for only those gone hog wild are blind to its priceless iridescence. As the saying goes, better a live hog than a dead lion. But who says this?

George Orwell's *Animal Farm* sets its literary teeth to liberal use in an allegorical chewing — a biting satire — of the false idol of Soviet Stalinism. The pigs in the novel are all — to a greater and lesser degree — representative of personalities involved in the early days of the Communist revolution, and its subsequent devolvement into a brutal dictatorship. The book is a strip of political bacon fried in its own grease, so to speak. The pigs running the farm are eventually barely distinguishable from the humans the animals originally revolted against, their great Commandment — "All animals are equal but some animals are more equal than others" — a betrayal of the revolution's earliest, and deepest, aspirations. And is that not so typically human? There is no doubt — we are swine.

Revolution is a state of affairs as familiar to me as my childhood, for before 1982 Bolivia counted more government changeovers than the number of years in its history. Whenever we saw tanks rolling down the highway outside the adobe walls of our schoolyard, we knew Bolivian politics were operating in the customary manner. For a country built on such chaos, it was a marvel anything functioned at all. And yet it did, though haltingly. And continues to do so, although perhaps not in a manner as seamlessly or efficiently as most of us would prefer, for we democratic Americans can be political snobs. Except, of course, we are not a pure democracy, but rather a federal republic also founded upon revolution. What does this mean? It means the British lost, we have no king (or queen), and rule ourselves through elected representatives operating within a structure which protects minority rights from the unrestrained will of the majority.

Good for America — and any place else which has some measure of governmental stability — but to the Christer, politics are not politic, for the Master has told us his kingdom is not of this world. Christ never chose a political path, for he spoke of spirit and truth. Our life is Personal and that Person is Christ. Politics should not be our primary concern — transforming votaries into voters — for it was not the Master's primary concern. (Our thoughts should mirror the mind of

God, not the god of the mind.) It is secondary to our citizenship in heaven, to our placement within the Body of Christ. A Christer owes allegiance to no man and no country, but to God alone in Christ. And yet a Christer pays required taxes, works diligently, cares for the poor, and promotes Christerica's own peculiar peace. Indeed, it appears the best resident a country could ever hope for is one who owes allegiance to a higher authority whose heavenly constitution requires silent worship, neighborly love, and humble service.

At one time, British Common Law included a now-obsolete provision called denizenship. The denizen was neither a citizen nor an alien, but something in between. The last denizen of Britain was Dutch painter Lawrence Alma-Tadema, a personal favorite of mine thanks to his glowing depictions of marble and stone, for I too am a paintsmith of sorts, obsessively partial to such winsome marmoreal renderings.

There is a secret to the luminance in Alma-Tadema's painted surfaces. It is a thing called subsurface scattering. One can easily experiment with this at home, after taking the necessary precautions and wearing the appropriate safety gear. Arrange something like an orange slice — or even an actual orange slice — on a stable surface in a dim room. (After all, as C.S. Lewis said, we live in the shadowlands.)[70] Now shine a light directly at the orange slice. You will see it much more clearly, but it will appear lifeless, merely an object clinically exposed.

But now shine the light upon the orange slice from behind, and one will see something amazing. The orange slice is illuminated. It comes to life, for the light is shining through it. The orange slice absorbs a certain amount of light, and transmits an inner essence to the viewer. This is subsurface scattering. (A similar effect can be observed by holding one's hand up to the light. The outer edges of the fingers will appear to glow.) So long as one paints with such illumination in mind, incredibly lifelike rendering can be achieved.

In the same manner, one illuminates the culture one inhabits through the same Christlike subsurface scattering, for we are semi-translucent beings and the light of the Master must shine through us. We glow along our edges, and like droplets of water levitating over a heated surface in the Leidenfrost effect, our interaction is a teflon-like engagement. For Christers are denizens of this world, not citizens. But if this is the case, one might say, how exactly do we interact in meaningful, productive ways within our social and political environment?

The artist Makoto Fujimura promotes a thing called culture care,[71] and it is a very fine thing. But I would step back a little further and call our function soul care, for politics and culture are worthless without soul. That is — in a sense — invalid. For the world in its natural state is essentially invalid in a spiritual sense. But Christ's reality has opened the possibility of validity in the eyes of God. But let us consider the words valid and invalid. We are all, after all, moral invalids. That is we are "not valid", not acceptable. In-valid. For the word valid derives form the Latin for strong, healthy, worthy. We are not that. Certainly not that. We are weak and we are not worthy. But this is exactly what we need to be, to be made worthy. For to be is not to be — there is no question. Indeed, Christerica is not for the healthy, but for the sick and the searching. Our invalidation is the prerequisite for our validation, for Christ only validates the invalid. Our admitted enervation is admission to Christ's healing ministration. This is our plaint-song of disease, our dirge of desperation. And no one comes to the Father but through hymn.

In a very real sense — and perhaps in the most ultimate sense — our Christer function here on earth is one of palliative care, for as I demonstrated with the Dental Proof, death salience is for real and our indentured servitude is for life. This is why a hardy kindness is so valuable, why tough love is a necessity. Everyone is dying, no one will question this. We are all spiritual invalids. Indeed, actual physical invalids too, for entropy does not take leave or go on vacation. The only question is how will we die, when will we die, and what happens after. What light can we bring to this darkness? To this we have an answer. The answer will not cure one's present disease or prevent one's temporal death — or even make one rich or happy — but it will, in hope, structure and guarantee one's eternal function.

The life-limiting illness we have is sin, literally the missing of the mark. Indeed, for many, the mark itself is missing. Nobody even knows what they are aiming at. For a lighthouse — though a beacon — is also a warning. The light is a guide, but approach at one's peril, for upon reaching it one will be wrecked upon its rock. And there is only one Rock and one remedy as far as we can understand, and that is belief in the salvific work of Christ. Some may see this mythologically or psychologically, but though both epistemological filters have positive merits, the true meaning is absolutely literal. One can be saved, all the way across time and space and beyond, for I have seen the subsurface scattering of the Spirit and its source is eternal and strong.

So then, palliative care with a difference — the offer of imperishable hope, a prescription for the universal PanChrista, a sort of cure-all Christic panacea. And if our ongoing palliative care brings some measure of shalom or human flourishing to this earth, that is only a byproduct of our denizenship on earth and our true citizenship in heaven. Playing musical chairs on a sinking ship is pointless unless indeed the music points less to the ship and more to the lifeboats.

If this world is all there is, if we are simply marvellously complicated iterations of time and causality, then there really is no hope, and no validity. All instinctively know this. Why else is the world full of religion? But religion is not the answer — religion is the question. Christ is the answer to religion. It is a sad and evil thing that the freedom of Christ has been transformed over time into mere religion. But that is the nature of our world, and subject for another chapter.

The Master did not fellowship with the existentially sick as an enabler, but as a healer. He is not a dealer in permission, but rather an agent of remission. Not a facilitator, but a felicitator, for he eulogizes the penitent, robbing the grave. For the grave's seriousness surrenders to the Master's joy.

The Master himself is the light shining through us, illuminating our true beauty and worth. We have lost our marbles, only to find them in the Master's hand transformed into pearls. And we are cast as they are cast.

And we, being indentured to the Master, are sound teeth with healthy roots. We are structurally instantiated, for as we masticate the Master, our appetites are transformed from the hoggish to the coggish. Like a fine set of indestructible dentures, we interlock fittingly, functioning appropriately and efficiently.

So let us be responsive. Let us be pearlworthy. And let us choose well as one who chews well.

For to quote Kierkegaard, "I would rather be a swineherd, understood by the swine, than a poet misunderstood by men."[72]

Pause and consider.

CHAPTER 19

ELEPHANT

<u>PARAFABULON</u>

After another late night of drinking and gambling in the village, a man returned home to find his wife waiting for him in their humble hut.

"The children are safely sleeping," she said. "Now it is urgent for you and I to speak of the elephant in the room."

The husband buried his face in his hands and said, "I know, I know; how many times have we spoken of this? Must we speak of it again? My drinking! My gambling! How often have I failed in my duties as a husband and a father? As a man! I have lost so much money and wasted so much time; but perhaps not, perhaps I too have feelings; perhaps I desire a life greater than that encompassed by these four miserable walls; who will be my judge? You? Perhaps, perhaps; in fact, certainly; and why not? why not indeed? you are well within your rights; we made vows; I admit, other women have their attractions, but how am I to blame? Having been born this way, it cannot be my fault, and yet it is; self-delusion and self-control rarely walk hand in hand; I am tethered to my vices and cannot walk hands-free; I wish I could, but I feel my heart beating; it betrays me; the world outside this domestic prison has captured my desire; I flee and fall; fall and fail; the money from the cookie jar — I took it; yes, I took it; do not look at me with such horror; but then maybe I am joking; or lying; yes, lying; no doubt I have lied to you more times than I have not; but even I suspect my lies of being untrue; how the promise of youth has curdled in the cup of life! If life is a bowl of cherries, why are we drinking lemonade? Nothing ever makes sense…"

The wife, who had been watching and listening to her husband with some astonishment, said, "Why do you speak of such things in such a manner?"

The husband said, "You desired that we must speak."

And the wife said, "No, I meant there is literally an elephant in the room. Right in front of you. Can you not see it?"

The husband raised his head and stared blindly in wonder, saying, "I cannot, for all is only grey."

RUMINATIO

Elephants are uncommonly large. This is not uncommon knowledge. In fact, elephants are so relentlessly immense it is counterintuitively possible for them to be virtually invisible. One cannot see the elephant for the elephant. How so, one may ask? If one's perspective is warped or one's focal depth calibrated incorrectly, or even if one is physically situated at a distance incommensurate with perceptual totality — that is, standing too close — such mass can appear in its abstract parts as undifferentiated viewscapes of indeterminate meaning. Indeed, there are times when the obvious is invisible, and the invisible equally obvious, for grey is only the undifferentiated mixing and muddying of black and white.

There is a well-known experiment — it can be viewed online — where groups of university students are asked to watch a video showing various people dressed in either black or white milling about in a confined space. There is a ball being passed back and forth between them. The watching university students are then asked to count how many times a member of the white team passes the ball to another member of the white team. What the watching university students do not know is the number of passes does not matter, for in the midst of their concentrated focus upon the passing of the ball, a figure fully clad in a black gorilla suit walks directly into the center of the frame, stops, waves at the viewer, and moves on.

The question is: how many of the watching university students notice the gorilla? The surprising answer is: only about half. What does this tell us? What conclusions can be drawn regarding human perception?

We could say we see what we are looking for, and do not see what we are not looking for. This has been given the name "attentional blindness", as one may remember from my earlier comments regarding birdwatching. Extreme attention to one thing is liable to blind us to many another thing. Indeed, the more capable one is of focused attention to detail, the more one is susceptible to blindness elsewhere. (We are all aware of the stereotype of the absent-minded professor, but he is actually not so much absent-minded, as attentionally blind, and more so than most, due to his extreme attention to one particular aspect of reality.) Not that the results of such supposedly unbiased pinpoint vision are false or untrue, they are simply partial in their purported impartiality. For life is more than the sum of its parts, and detail is only meaningful in the context of... well, context.

Sadhu Sundar Singh — wandering Indian mystic and faithful follower of the Master — once told the story of a scientist who wished to find the life of a bird, and where it might be located in the bird's body.[73] In dissecting the bird, the life for which he was searching mysteriously vanished. The Sadhu said, "Those who try to understand the inner life merely intellectually will meet with a similar failure. The life they are looking for will only vanish." Indeed, all life disappears when deconstructed, for life is in the construction. It is systemic and systematic. It is somehow a thing greater than the sum of its parts. Life, not surprisingly, is found only in the living.

In the same way, moving pictures become movies, for the still life of a single frame is still greater life when multiplied in time. Indeed, the high degree of animation convinces our senses and emotions that something resembling life — perhaps even more vivid than life — is taking place, a meaningful dramatic rendering of some portion of our existential plight.

As a child I frequented various cinemas throughout Cochabamba, for not only were they congenial venues of magical visual narration, but from the moment I chose my seat at the ticket booth — purchasing the rolled up ticket stuffed into the little hole drilled on a board representing the floor plan of the theatre — to the flickering of the projector in the raucous darkness, they were theaters for the intensely social interchange of conversation and ideas. The lobby would be filled with friends and enemies alike, banter and insults were traded there and in the seats, and the monophrastic candy vendors (*"Chicle!" "Chancaca!"*) would ply the aisles with trays of goodies platforming out from their waists, suspended by leather straps slung around the back of their necks.

I remember well — speaking of elephants and Indian mystics — a very gripping, emotional Indian film which at one point featured an elephant so sad that tears poured from its eyes and down its pachydermal grey skin. I did not know whether elephants were capable of crying or not, but the Spanish subtitles gave me no cause to doubt, for subtitles were the supplementary means of further comprehension. Indeed, many of my friends learned English from watching American movies whose Spanish subtitles gave them the keys to the language dramatized before their very eyes.

In a similar manner, Scripture provides the subtitles to the inner life of the Christer, for Christerica is mute in the earthly realm without language to describe and share it. After all, to witness is not to convince, but to relate the details of a story in such a manner as to at least attempt to transmit the basic outline and meaning.

Then, as now, though some liked going to church, more loved going to movies. For we hunger for narrative like a beggar for bread. We eat story and live by words. The Master himself says it is the very words from the mouth of God which give us life. The limited visions of the theater implicitly suggest a higher vision which transcends our current reality, for such things are only possible if they are grounded in possibility. The Christer, then, is the ultimate possibility thinker. And Christerica is our ultimate possibility.

For there is something happening here in our existence which we do not understand fully, or even partially, but which Christerica comes the closest to revealing in its most crucial elements. We exist on the only planet in the entire universe — so far as we know — which has liquid water and observable life. But not just some water — lots of it. And not just some life — but an incredible multiplicity of it.

The universe is not friendly to life of any kind. What miracle is this that we are here, existing — nay, thriving — under this sheet of breathable gas, tucked under this thin blanket pulled over our heads against the vast interstellar chill, conscious of our selves? It cannot be chance; it cannot be random. What does it mean? This is the universal question. Every one of us born into this life asks the same questions: what does it mean?

Why are we here? For we could just as easily — nay, more easily — not be here. And yet this question is unanswerable, for we do not have the means or knowledge to answer it on our own recognizance. But it must have an answer, for why would we ask it? Why? Why? This is our appeal and our lament.

At the same time, we struggle for survival, knowing full well we will all die regardless of the success or failure of that struggle. But we cannot come to terms with this, for our desire to live is too strong and the details of our material existence too overpowering and seemingly too fraught with incipient meaning. Truly, we live in denial of death, for that same denial is the basic prerequisite of the ability to function in any perceptibly or partially meaningful way. This is what we call life. Small wonder we hunger for story as one thirsting for water in an endless desert, for story narrates meaning and justifies drama. We are insatiable, for story is humanity's most basic sustenance, the temporary assurance that all this "degraded clowning" (thanks, Saul Bellow)[74] is not simply a joke.

Into this dream — into this madness, into this vast existential conspiracy — steps the Master, making claims only the Creator of this drama could make. And the claims state that there is meaning, and that this meaning is in him, if we will only trust in him. He assures us there is life beyond this life — or rather, death — just as we had always hoped, suspected, and imagined. That this dying struggle we live is not without consequence or meaning. That all stories tell something true.

That these hands and minds uniquely built for technology and teleology are meant to be used. That things are actually something. And that everything is not just nothing.

The Master has opened a Gate. A narrow Gate. We do not truly know what is beyond the Gate. We can only walk through it by the faith given to us by the grace of the Master. So then: if we have faith, let us live in grace. And if we are given grace, let us live by faith. And if we have neither, let us pray for both, for our prayers are a sort of sub-belief floating upon our unbelief. As the man says in Scripture, "Lord, I believe, help thou mine unbelief."[75] For Christ himself is the Gate. We must walk in him and through him for our narratives to come true, and for our stories to have meaning. For our lives are rendered believable by external confirmation, and such confirmation can only come from a higher authority.

But is there objectivity? Is there a place we can stand and make judgments? Yes and no. Yes, in the sense that the Christer stands on the solid rock of Christ in faith; no, in the sense that, for us — as we actually experience life — all is in constant motion. Our hope is in tension, for a slack tightrope is difficult to tread upon. Tension is required for balance.

Movies are vast and complicated metaphors which we inhabit for a short period of time to experience their symbolic weight. In like manner, I for many years inhabited a metaphor called "windsurfing". Those who know me will laugh, for they will only believe I was having fun. Indeed, I will not lie — I was enjoying myself. But the enjoyment was of a peculiar sort.

Of course there were the technical details: the wind speeds, pressure gradients, sale shapes, fin foils, carbon fiber components, millimetres of wetsuit thickness, and so on. But these were the secular scriptures, the instructional subtitles. The life of the metaphor was, like a movie, in the motion generated by the tension and interaction between various forces.

The writer of Ecclesiastes saw that all things done under the sun were meaningless, a chasing after the wind.[76] But chasing after the wind is not meaningless if wind is precisely that which one chases. Indeed, Scripture itself likens the Holy Spirit to a rushing wind, and Christers as those who move like the wind. Wind is life, and like a movie, it moves. Wind is the movement of air, and air carries the oxygen we need to breath and speak. Therefore, when I say windsurfing is a spiritual metaphor, perhaps it will not simply sound like blowing wind. Homer said, "Words empty as the wind are best left unsaid." But who listens to ancient Greek poets? Perhaps his own words are empty. But words are never empty, and neither is the wind. Both have content, and are content to be both, for words are simply wind given shape.

Consider that in life everything is in motion, for, again, motion is life. Everything is in motion, and so are we. Even the hermit in his desert cell cannot avoid the downward glide of entropy, the onward flow of time, or the metronomic movement of the heart. Everything is in motion. This is made clear in the most tangible way possible in windsurfing. More precisely, high-wind/small-board windsurfing. For without movement, the board will sink, and without sufficient wind in the sail, the board will not move. One is faced with active water, a fluid medium compounded of wave and current over which one has no control. Over the wind, one also has no control, for it is an overwhelming force exhibiting often inconsistent levels of speed and surprising multidirectional gusts.

Amongst these gargantuan powers — as in life — one could easily be lost, for how small is man when suspended between an omnipotent God and the massed forces of the universe? Indeed, in many instances such a combination could be lethal, and often is. And yet with skill, the appropriately sized sail, and a sailboard of suitable dimensions, one may be able to improvise upon the situation in such a way that one not only harnesses the power of the wind, but also traverses the watery terrain in a manner which not only produces movement, but which enables one to fairly fly across the surface with not only miraculous speed, control, and maneuverability, but also a sense of purpose and direction, for it is crucial to maintain one's positioning on tacks and reaches so as to be able to return to one's launch point.

One would think this might be sufficient depth already for a metaphor to measure, as all of the factors mentioned above clearly mirror the life of the Christer in regards to this world. I will not insult the intelligence of the reader by spelling everything out. But there are also wetsuits, flotation devices, helmets, gloves, and the like which all carry allusive resonance to various elements of spiritual armor we may choose to wear in the course of our spiritual sailing. And not only that, there is the added concept of "laylines". (Not to be confused with "ley lines", ancient lines or pathways connecting sacred structures or significant landforms thought to have spiritual significance. Although, yes, those lines as well, but I am talking about windsurfing.)

A layline in windsurfing is essentially an imaginary line between the sailor and a distant landmark which aids in navigation across the changeable — both featureful and featureless — surface of the water. For just as with the elephant, one cannot see what one needs to see without the proper perspective, the forest for the trees, the painting for the paint, even the Church for the Christians. The Christer has Christ as landmark and Scripture as layline, the nature of the wind (Spirit) ahead being read by the experienced sailor on the surface of the water (life) like the page of a book. Thus we stay on the right tack and keep the board on a balanced and effective plane. *Selah.*

It has been said all religions of the world are like blind men touching the elephant of ultimate truth. Each mistakes their part for the whole. This is often put forward as a supposedly devastating critique of those who claim ultimate truth. But metaphors — as with elephants — can be misleading and easily run rampant, for who says ultimate truth is an elephant, and that religions are blind men? Only those who create such metaphors in the first place, for it begs the question. In a similar manner, an elephant with its tail in its trunk finds it difficult to walk or look ahead. Why would it do this? For no reason other than foolishness. This is not wisdom, neither is it vision. Such metaphorical posturing deployed as supposedly self-evident neutral epistemology is exposed as bias, for it is simply grasping its own tale and therefore cannot manage any meaningful narrative headway. In truth, it is that very bias which is the elephant in the room, for it is making the very claim to ultimate knowledge which it pretends to critique. Indeed, as a Christer, one could just as easily say that Christerica is the elephant which the blind of every earthly religion can only partially comprehend, for even the wildest native in the deepest jungle seems to have a partial premonition of this dimly understood reality whose fragmentary details are yet clearly visible.

There are times when the possible seems likely, and the likely becomes certain. Gold miners in early America who returned east to their homes after a failed attempt to strike a fortune out west were wont to say, "I saw the elephant." That is, they saw their hopes and dreams trampled by reality. So too is every possible religion — including often "Christianity" itself — trampled by the certain reality of Christ, for Christ destroys every likely illusion of the sacred and every presumption of the religious.

A white elephant is the term given to something too costly for its minimal usefulness. Such is Christerica, for what profit is there in gaining one's soul if one must forfeit the world, some might say? The Scriptures never mention whether the Master laughed, but he certainly wept. He is the crying elephant in every room, our crying elephant, and a white one at that. For there is no grey in Christ, and following him is too costly for our worldly usefulness. For he is not "useful" at all and cannot be made to fit into our shortsighted earthly schemes. He is the square peg to the round hole of every religion and political ideal, and we — as we come round — are made square.

And Christerica, body of square parts, like the contents of a still, is distilled and purified, for by removing the diluting effects of sin the proportion of spirit is increased, and the lives of every constituent Christer becomes a sanctified frame in a four-dimensional moving picture.

For the Master is always on the move, and we also. For we move in the Master's movies — in truth, we are the Master's movies — and these movies are truly moving.

In this colossal theater of darkness, we have seen the Light.

And in light of that Light, we have truly seen the Elephant. And been trampled.

But such transcendent trampling is the provenance of the Master's new wine.

Pause and consider.

CHAPTER 20

ARMADILLO

PARAFABULON

An armadillo said to a toucan, "There are no meaningful parables in the entire world about armadillos."

"Few with toucans, either," said the toucan.

"Not even Aesop had much use for us," said the armadillo. "Imagine that. Us."

"Right? Look at us," said the toucan. "You with the amazing shell; me with the huge, colorful beak."

"But that is all we really have," said the armadillo. "I mean, to be honest, our personalities are not the most interesting."

"And human interaction is very low," said the toucan. "I can be captured as a pet, but nothing really happens. They just put me in a cage and look at me. Feed me some fruit. I make a mess. Act crabby. Sound terrible."

"And they just use my shell to make those little guitars," said the armadillo. "What are they called?"

"I do not know," said the toucan, "And frankly do not care. But at that point you are dead anyhow — not much of an interaction!"

"No," said the armadillo, "I am not really a fan of drama anyhow. I just ball up."

"Well, there you go," said the toucan. "No drama; no parable. You cannot have one without the other."

"But drama is trauma," said the armadillo, almost rolling up into a ball at the very thought.

"Right?" said the toucan. "Who wants drama? Not me."

"Still," said the armadillo, "there must be something; some way we can be parabolically relevant."

The armadillo and the toucan pondered this riddle in silence for some time.

The armadillo ate a grub.

The toucan ate a banana.

No parable in sight.

Finally the toucan said, "One thing I suspect — if one of us could discover a relevant moral which would make a parable workable, they would surely name it after that one."

"I like that idea," said the armadillo. "I really do."

"It is very difficult, though," said the toucan. "I mean, I have seen myself on a cereal box. Is that a thing? Could that be a thing?"

"I do not know," said the armadillo. "The thing is, we do not have much, but what little we have is taken away. And others, who already have a lot, they seem to get more."

The toucan and the armadillo stared at each other.

"Congratulations," said the toucan, and flew away.

RUMINATIO

We once owned a toucan. I say owned, but I truly do not know where it came from or why it became our responsibility. Perhaps, in the nature of the Bolivian *anticrético* real estate transaction mentioned earlier in this book, it came with that particular property. In any case, the toucan was housed in a massive, free-standing, Gothic-looking, wrought-iron silo located on the concrete of the courtyard at the back of our residence.

This was the same patch of courtyard where I fell upon my head once after losing consciousness on account of hanging upside down from a bar above the concrete too soon after sitting inside reading a book. One may be familiar with such rising-to-the-feet-too-quickly blackouts. But pause and consider: I blacked out, then pitched onto my head and was furtherly knocked unconscious. This seemed fundamentally unfair, an embarrassment of pitches. However, as the

Scriptures say, "For whosoever hath, to him shall be given, and he shall have more abundance: but whosoever hath not, from him shall be taken away even that he hath."[77] *Selah*.

The toucan of which I was speaking was a mean, aggressive bird, murderously clashing its colorful beak against the blackened bars in an effort to take off one's fingers if they strayed anywhere near. This toucan was messy, unapologetically wild, and seemingly vindictive. Perhaps it was justified in this behaviour. I do not know, for I had no knowledge of its history. But perhaps if one were a toucan, one would act in a similar manner given the circumstances. Again, I do not know. However, one day it managed to escape. Our dogs — for we had two at the time — promptly killed and ate it. There may be a lesson here. Pause and consider.

However, at this present moment I am armadillo-prioritized, for we also owned an armadillo. I say we, as in one of my sisters, and armadillo, as in the shell of one forming the rounded body of the soundbox on the instrument she played. This instrument was called a *charango*. What is a *charango*? It is a very small ten-stringed guitar native to Bolivia, made (in part) from the carapace of an armadillo.

For those unfamiliar with the armadillo, it is — more or less — a rabbit with a protective shell: sometimes more, sometimes less, depending upon what that might mean in regards to one's perspectival epistemology. That is, from one angle — let us call it the shell angle — an armadillo is not like a rabbit at all, but from another — imagine fur in place of shell — it is very much like a rabbit. In fact, a little further north, the Aztecs literally called the armadillo a "turtle-rabbit". (*Azotochtli.*)

One may well wonder why this unique animal was not mentioned earlier in the chapter on rabbits and turtles, for it seems almost the perfect synthesis of the two, brimming with symbolic richness as a Christer metaphor, for what is Christ but two realities in one, an eternal Word incarnated, the Logos written in meat? One can only say the mind has its reasons of which the heart knows nothing, and that a suit of armor is heavier than a wetsuit, and that an armadillo can float in water by self-inflation, or sink to the bottom and ford bodies of water by simply walking and holding its breath. It seems the weight of its armor is not as constricting as one might imagine, and neither is ours. *Selah.*

Indeed, an armadillo can run like a rabbit and, similar to a turtle, hide inside its shell for protection. It can jump (up to four feet straight into the air), swim (it is actually a type of crustacean), and sing (as in making sounds with its mouth completely unlike singing). The Spanish coined the word *armadillo*, which means "little armoured one". The indigenous Bolivian Quechua people call it a *khirkinchu*. The indigenous Bolivian Aymara people call it a *khirkhi*. This means whatever they want it to mean, for the Quechua and Aymara — descendants of the Incas — deserve whatever linguistic freedom they desire after having been exploited for so many centuries. Indeed, my parents' work of helping translate the entire Bible into Quechua was part of an attempt to promote literacy in the here and now, and possibly expand their freedom into the now and then of the metaphysical realm apart from the traditionally oppressive authorities, worldly and otherwise.

And yet there are times when one suspects these colorful autochthon of playing some species of long game which those of us who see the future as being in front of us might not understand, for the Quechua and Aymara understand time as a visible spatial dimension. In other words, the past — not the future — is in front of one. One can only see the past, never the future. The future is behind one and one can only cautiously back into it as one views what has gone before in front of one. To the Incan and post-Incan mind, traveling through time is like driving a vehicle with one's eyes on the rearview mirror. Pause and consider when traveling by Bolivian public transport.

Of course, in the interim, these differing cultural perceptions of time could well be what gave rise to the armadillo-bodied *charango* in the first place. For in the typical Western mindset, because one looks ahead, one is always imaginatively extrapolating into the future. Thus, to one, a featureless, pyramidal, high-altitude Bolivian mountain devoid of vegetation may seem materially insignificant, while to another, it might hold untold riches given time, mining know-how, and the means of excavation. And free labor.

I am speaking, of course, about the Bolivian city of Potosí and the mountain above it called *Cerro Rico* (Rich Mountain). Today, Potosí is a small town with a number of poor inhabitants scratching a meagre living mining traces of tin from the once-fabulous mountain. But there was a time when Potosí was larger than Paris, for the *Cerro Rico* was the largest-yielding silver and tin mine in history. The Spanish plundered it for all it was worth, using the aboriginal peoples essentially as slaves, many millions of whom died in the process. It was during this time, it seems, the indigenous population appropriated some form of the Spanish guitar and created the *charango* using, instead of wood — which was not perhaps readily available, and required much time and effort to shape — the shells of dead armadillos.

I will not wade too much farther into the controversy of the true origins of this instrument, or the word *charango* itself, for the reader may well imagine there are those more expert in these matters than myself, and the reader's imagining would not be far wrong. But perhaps the *charango* could be viewed as the ultimate symbol of protest and hope, for it is as if the indigenous people are saying, "Yes, you have taken the armadillo of our being, killed it, eviscerated it, and renovated our shell with the superstructure of Spanish culture — as you have with much else in our land — but we, though looted, will yet use this luted amalgam to make music of our own, not only despite this ungodly splicing, but because of it. And we also add panpipes. And cowhide drums." This dynamite combination may yet move mountains traditional explosives never could.

The armadillo, when threat is perceived, famously rolls into a ball. One must see this to believe it, for it happens very quickly, and the result is much more compact and smoothly spherical than one would imagine. It becomes literally a perfect ball. Turtles must hate them. So jealous. But this rolling/unrolling action always brings to this one's mind the yo-yo, that inescapable toy which almost every kid from almost every culture has seen or played with in some form — as I have — for it was invented over five hundred years before Christ. Indeed, I have often wondered what sort of toys Jesus himself might have had when he was a boy. The disciples and early apostles obviously did not think toys worthy of Scriptural mention, but one cannot help wonder: did Christ every play with toys? Did he have a yo-yo? And was he skilled with it?

I have a nephew who wonders if he could defeat Jesus at basketball, playing one-on-one. It would be an interesting contest, one upon which I myself would not wager money or presume to build any form of doctrine, for though Christ himself was not familiar with basketball, he was an inspired parabolist, and what more is the arc of a shot in basketball than a type of parabola? It could well transpire that Christ would transform the entire contest into a winning parable not in my nephew's favor, or he might simply turn the tables by saying, "He that is without sin, let him cast the first shot." And since they would be playing possession, it is hard to imagine what sort of defence could be played thereafter, for Christ might say, "Only the proud raise their hands against their God," or "A scoundrel goes around shuffling the feet."

However, in Christ all things are possible.

A yo-yo is a fascinating contrivance for it gains from gravity the very means to defeat gravity. What I mean to say is, the throw plus gravity creates enough of what is called "rotational inertia" to defy gravity on the way back up. My sons often ask me what sort of toys I owned as a child in Bolivia. I invariably tell them our familial poverty only allowed for one stick and one rock. This, of course, is not true, though deeply amusing to everyone not other than myself. Indeed, I also played with sand, dead leaves, and broken glass. (Still they do not laugh.)

Honesty compels me to admit there was more: a frisbee, soccer ball, basketball, toy cars and trucks, even a Slinky. I loved the Slinky, for it seemed magical and mysterious that a simple coil of wire could come to life in such a manner, given only a few descending steps and the law of gravity. Moreover, the Slinky afforded even further fascination, for the enigmatic inventor of that very toy occasionally worked with my father in Cochabamba at the "print shop" — a densely active suite of rooms redolent of ink and paper, enchanted with trays of metal letters, and aggressively noisy with the incessant clattering of intricate machinery — where all sorts of Quechua literacy materials were produced. (As previously mentioned.)

But in Bolivia there were existential stairs aplenty, and gravity enough to draw one's mortal coil in directions not altogether reasoned or reasonable. *Selah*. The head may wish to follow the heart, but the heart also has reason to follow the head, for to pitch headlong into precipitous commitment may be harmful, and the innocently impulsive may be disastrously divulsive. This I myself found when I naively modified my Slinky in hopes of improved performance, only to find it hopelessly bent and stretched in such a manner that it could no longer navigate even the most simple of stairways, causing it to tumble haplessly to the bottom. Indeed, the concrete of reality may easily concuss even the most well-meaning wayfarer if one misses critical steps.

So then: let us be like the yo-yo whose rotational inertia is not unguided, and whose body not only falls, but rises again.

Let us be the *charango*, but never the pan flute, for now is not the time for hot air, but for strumming life.

Let us even be the Slinky, but only in perpetual motion on the Master's ascending escalator, for then our inexorable downward motion will be overcome and gravity will no longer be our master.

However, even better than all that, let us be more than careless converts, toys, or *charangos*. Let us be like living armadillos in our faith, little armored ones who can both float and sink, but still walk. Brave, yes, but careful and full of care.

For in our flexibly protective shells we will surely roll.

Pause and consider.

CHAPTER 21

WOLF

PARAFABULON

A wolf followed three little pigs to their home.

He knocked on the door, but the pigs would not open it.

"Little pigs, little pigs, let me in!"

"Not by the hair of our chinny-chin-chins!"

"Then I will…"

The wolf stopped.

"Will what?" he said to himself. "Huff and puff?"

He stood there for some time shaking his head and pondering. He had read some books. He knew the tale.

"If I do not change the story," said the wolf to himself, "I will end up going down the chimney into the cauldron of boiling water, just as I have read of wolves before me."

The wolf reviewed the facts: "The wolf in the story blew the straw house down; the pigs ran to the stick house. The wolf in the story blew the stick house down; the pigs ran to the brick house. That's a lot of huffing and puffing and running around just to get to the brick house, which spells doom for me anyhow. There must be another way out of this endless recursion."

The wolf was well aware that his namesake had employed many crafty tricks to capture the pigs outside their home. None of which worked.

Then an idea came to the wolf.

The wolf said, "Little pigs, little pigs!"

The pigs said, "Not gaining entry to our digs!"

The wolf said, "No, no — you do not understand. I did not come to rhyme, or even to climb. And to be honest, if I did want to dine, it would not be upon your fair pinkness, for I now identify as a pig myself. Worry no longer, my friends, I will be returning to my own home. I can only hope and pray that no wolves will bother me there. May you and I all live in peace, each in our own way."

And the wolf returned to his home.

The pigs were amazed and relieved.

"Just think," said one, "our lifelong enemy is now one of us."

"Not that we have to be friends with him," said the second.

"True," said one, "but to be honest, I feel a little rude not letting him in, now that we are all pigs together."

"I still think this is some sort of trick," said the third.

"Maybe it is and maybe it is not," said the second. "I do not care. We will simply ignore him."

"I am going to feel quite bad doing that," said the one. "It would be terribly discourteous."

"Oh my goodness," said the second. "Just leave it alone."

"Wait, though," said the third pig, "if it is a trick, we cannot just ignore him, for he might still attack us when we are out of the house. And if it is not a trick, it can only mean something worse, for a wolf is a wolf no matter what he may think at the moment. The only way this can ever end well is if we eliminate him forever, just as the stories have always foretold. And since we cannot simply stay inside this brick house, waiting for nothing, we must therefore go on the offensive. I have a plan."

After much discussion, argument, and rough planning, the pigs set off for the wolf's house disguised as wolves themselves, and heavily armed with pistols. Their appearance was really quite fierce.

They banged on the wolf's door.

"Little pig, little pig, let us in!" said the pigs.

"Not by the hair of my chinny-chin-chin!" said the wolf.

"Then we will huff, and we will puff, and we will blow your house in," said the pigs.

"Oh, no need for that," said the wolf, quickly opening the door. Surprised and startled, the pigs prepared to fire their weapons, but the wolf easily disarmed and captured them.

"We have been tricked!" said the pigs. "The wolf will eat us!"

But the wolf said, "Actually, yes to the first, but no to the second. Yes, you have been tricked, but no, I will not eat you, for I have made a decision to explore a vegan lifestyle. No more huffing and puffing and chimney-stuffing for me!"

And he took them to market to be sold as bacon.

RUMINATIO

I must confess having had very little to do with wolves in the course of my travels — or even over the course of my life — though upon further reflection my suspicions have been aroused — and perhaps even confirmed — that many of the apparent sheep interactive in my personal history were likely wolves in disguise. But I may be speaking metaphorically, as the case may be, for the chaos and confusion of our cultural moment is enough to bewilder even wolves, never mind the sheep they thought they were, or were pretending to be.

Transformation and identity are twin funnels of the dizzying and destructive tornadoes destabilizing our present personal and political climate, as can be easily observed through current events. Of course, none of this is truly new, for the earth has seen many a destructive ideology propagate upon its surface in its eons-long progression through space and time. Indeed, like idiosyncratic and undependable second-hand vehicles arrayed on a used car lot, any of these pre-owned persuasions and hand-me-down dogmas may easily be acquired — with or without approved financing, it seems — and driven wildly through the well-ordered streets of any civilization, creating confusion and turmoil — even death — until finally crashing into the walls of immutable fact and intransigent reality. But I was speaking of wolves.

Wolves surprise me, for they are much larger than one would think. Or, at least, than I would have thought, having never seen one in comparison to other similar creatures. We all have our preconceptions and misconceptions. I suppose it is their dog-like appearance which led me to this faulty perception, for one is often misled by familiar impressions. But in truth — now that my eyes have been opened and a thorough soul-searching complete — wolves are massive, hairy, and horrifying. And there is something in the symmetrical proportions of their facial features — especially that knowing gleam in the eyes — which gives one the intuition of almost human intelligence. No surprise, then, their storied use in folk tales, for they seem not only physically dangerous, but frighteningly canny, as if they were truly conscious and suspiciously malevolent.

Humans and wolves have had a long history together, for their various territorial expansions have always created some level of interspecies conflict. And in the course of time — given the human penchant for story, the impact of Christianity upon pagan culture, and the apparent realities of certain strange, sinister, and inexplicable events — the concept of the lycanthrope arose, the wolf-person, the man-wolf. This, of course, is our now-familiar werewolf, the creature able to morph from man to wolf, and back again. I have read that as recently as the eighteenth century, there were places in the Bavarian Alps where people continued to believe such things. This does not surprise me, for even in the very town in which I currently exist, there are those who still suspect the earth is flat. However, transformation and identity have a long narrative history. And it certainly has not ended, for it seems we continue to be inexplicably obsessed not only with werewolves, but also vampires, zombies, and all manner of the undead.

I am no Sigmund Freud or Carl Jung, but I have heard they had much to say about such things — some of it true, some of it mistaken, much of it obscure. However, were I to delve deeply into such matters, this book would cease to function in the manner set forth. Even the most marginally sane can observe this to be true. Therefore I will glide silently over the deep and turbulent depths of shadow, persona, anima and animus, the collective unconscious, individuation, id, ego, superego, and the like, straying not into such charted and uncharted waters, but rather sailing forthrightly towards topics of a more personal preference. Like Scripture.

By Scripture, I mean what many simply call "The Bible", the collection of books representing the textual foundation of the

Christer faith. (And some may argue the foundation of Western civilization in its entirety, for the Biblical narratives are as deeply meaningful as one will allow, seemingly bottomless in their power to explicate theology and psychology alike, maybe even history.)

The Bible is in many ways wolf-like, its impact larger than most would think, dangerous, life-altering, a book like no other book, its manifold inner cross-referencing an overwhelming hyper-linked fur. Even more, perhaps, it is a werewolf, a weretext, a werebook, for Christ himself is the wereword, the man-Logos, the man-text, the Word made flesh, God's creative word in human form. A strange beast, this Christ, this Bible. A sheep in wolves' clothing. This, a sort of lycanthropic literature. Deadly, but uniquely revenant, capable of transforming the lifeless into the most noble and human living thing possible, the alchemy of spiritual lead into gold. Indeed, ours is a sort of spiritual vampirism, for it is the blood of Christ which gives us life, and we are dead yet alive as we feed upon him.

Some will say all this is too fanciful, too miraculous, too supernatural. However, Christers by their very nature are supernatural, for our very existence is founded upon miracle. After all, the supernatural is simply the incomprehensibly natural. For suppose what we call "The Bible" is simply a supernatural literary production inspired by the Holy Spirit, a unique type of genre, a meta-book, a blend of fiction and non-fiction, myth and fact? It is not always a simple matter to determine what is historical and what is ahistorical, what is allegorical and what is metaphorical, what is categorical and what is oratorical. For the Master himself spoke in riddles and parables, a unique genre itself, deployed — in the Master's own words — as a means of mystification as much as explication. For parables feature a unique sort of ambiguous clarity. That is, their language is clear, but their meaning complex. They derive, after all, from a type of Jewish riddle called a *mashal*. And every *mashal* has a *nimshal*, a sort of spiritual interpretation. However, we are very low on *nimshal* these days.

There used to be a time when one could warn — or be warned — about wolves in sheep's clothing. But that time has passed. These days, even followers of the Master himself seem to be easily deceived by straight-up wolves, for some say a wolf — whether born that way or not — should be free to live out that wolfness to whatever personal limit desired. After all, a wolf is only the innocent victim of its own birth. What gives the hunter the right to judge the wolf, even if it is actively malevolent? This is the nonsense we live with. How has it come to this? Where has all the simple wisdom gone? The inability to discern correctly in light of popular culture is exactly the problem, for popular culture has always been a poor light by which to judge anything.

There are many in the so-called Christian world who, fancying themselves intellectuals, approach their own belief-text with a contradictory admixture of smug, superior criticism, and subsequent admonitory promotion. "There is no God," they say, "but we know God is love." "There is no salvation," they say, "but we know Christ is our Savior." "There is no sin," they say, "but we know evil when we see it."

The story is told of a young man who spoke very highly of his father, for to him his father seemed noble and true, his advice fine and good.

But a village elder well known for his lack of character warned him, saying, "I know your father. He is ill-informed, given to inaccuracies, and altogether unreliable."

"If this be the case," said the young man, "how should I live, and to whom shall I turn for advice?"

The village elder said, "Trust your elders."

"Which one?" said the young man.

"Ah," said the village elder, "the one most trustworthy."

"And so I will," said the young man, "for I am also a student of numbers. You and your advice are a double negative whose positive equals my father. Thank you for confirming my direction."

Whereupon the village elder bit his own hand in frustration. (For this was the custom in those parts.)

The Christer resorts to Scripture, for though Scripture does not say much about some things, it says much about other things. And the things it says much about are the things that matter. At least to the Christer, for the Christer is a projection of those very Scriptures as illuminated by the light of the Spirit of God.

Many read Scripture too literally, and yet not literally enough. Claims for inerrancy clash against those of myth. But here I introduce — please forgive me — yet another Christer protocol: Scripture must be taken more literally than the inerrantists, and less literally than the mythicists. All at the same time, meaningfully layered. How so, one may ask?

I earn a large part of my living as a painter. I work in pigment, color, texture, various media, and so on. When I create a special effect for a client's wall, ceiling, or pillar, it is achieved through a build-up of semi-translucent layers which, when seen all at once, overlaid in this manner, convinces the eye of the desired effect. In the same way, I layer my art panels with marble dust slurries, dry pigments, various binders, isolating coats, protective coats, and so on. The final effect is highly wrought, yet not completely explicable. Every portion is detailed and essential to the final effect, and yet for all its singularity, that portion, though crucial, is not the entire painting. Indeed, it is absolutely necessary, yet dependent for its effect upon the concerted effort of every other detail on view.

Perhaps the Bible operates in similar manner to an abstract painting (though one which includes elements of collage, surrealism, and even hyper-realist figuration). Every part of it is real and inspired, certainly, but what does it mean? And what do its parts mean? The Bible as it is — in the form we have it now — is to my mind a work of art inspired by the process of the Holy Spirit. And fallible humans are part of that process. It has taken the form necessary for it to express what it is meant to express. Understanding this expression requires attention and interaction. Which is exactly the point, just as with an abstract painting. It is a challenge for every one of us, for as a priesthood of believers, it is for every one of us to understand it the best we can and stand upon that interpretation, and stand in that light. And, of course, as with any great work of art, we are judged by it, more than it is judged by us, no matter how we may falsely congratulate ourselves upon the critical value of our interpretive capacities.

But the one very important thing one cannot do is deny the presence of some element of the painting. Or, let us say, Scripture. One cannot Marcion-or-Thomas-Jefferson-cut-and-paste with the Bible, just as one cannot likewise mutilate a piece of art without a reduction in fulness and meaning. (Never mind Banksy!) One cannot look at a Van Gogh sunflower painting and say, "It appears there are sunflowers, but since I do not feel they add anything to the painting — and I do not believe in sunflowers anyway — I will say they are not there. Or at least not meant to be there. Or if apparently there, Van Gogh did not mean them to appear as sunflowers. The brushstrokes and color which apparently make up the sunflower effect are only so accidentally. Van Gogh actually meant something else." As if the image could not be both brushstroke and flower simultaneously. For that is exactly what painting is. And so with words.

I have heard it denied that the story of Pinocchio is about a wooden puppet wishing to become a real boy. Instead, it is a mythological rendering of a psychological exploration into the nature of being. Yes. It is. Both. These are layers. And one cannot do away with one, without doing away with the other. They exist in synchrony.

In the same way, one cannot deny an element of Scripture just for the reason that it does not fit one's interpretive scheme. One cannot in good conscience impose an interpretive scheme upon the text which excludes an interpretive layer, for this is a totalitarian approach whose consequence can only cause harm and confusion. Instead, one must holistically layer one's interpretive scheme upon all other interpretive schemes, one upon the other, embracing the totality of the work. For in this way, the richness of the text is enhanced and bodies forth its import. (Followed by its export.) For one cannot say — as an example — God (or Christ for that matter) is without wrath simply because one wishes to say God is without wrath, for God's wrath is spoken of frequently throughout Scripture, as is His love. Indeed, His love is only meaningful in the context of His wrath. At most one may attempt to reinterpret what God's wrath might mean, or how it might work itself out in the fields of justice, mercy, and love, but one cannot deny it is there, for it is a crucial part of the composition. The same could be said for matters of eternal judgment, spiritual gifts, practical directives, and so on.

These are simple matters, yet many have immense difficulty with them, for their minds are inelastic and unimaginative. Or, sometimes, though imaginative, they are corrupt. But the Christer trusts in the transformation of the weretext, for Christ is the wereword, leader of the spiritual pack, head of the transcendent Body.

And in many ways the Christer is the transformative lone wolf who is yet capable of pack activity. The pack, or local assembly, is a mode of existence available to the wolf, but the lone wolf attends to its own concerns. Of course, this is only a very rough equivalency to a Christer, for Christers are not only lone wolves, but perhaps black sheep as well, for a Christer does not play or exist according to pack rules or — as has been said — herd mentality. And yet, even so, lone wolves are yet wolves, and black sheep, sheep.

So then: in the absence of the Shepherd, the mature sheep must be wolf enough to guard the flock, for the incorporation of our inner wolf gives us the strength to be the sheep we must become.

Never cry, wolf. For tears are a sign of morning, but we illuminate the darkness, for — as the Russian proverb says — when night falls the face of the wolf lights up.

Pause and consider.

CHAPTER 22

FOX (AND COYOTE)

PARAFABULON

Driven by hunger, a fox attempted to reach some grapes hanging high upon the vine, but could not.

"Oh, you sour grapes!" said the fox. "I did not want you anyway."

"What?" said the grapes. "Who said that? Who disturbs the shrine of the vine?"

"I," said the fox.

"Sour grapes obviously do not make sweet whine, in your case," said the grapes.

"What are you talking about?" said the fox.

"The sweetest grapes hang highest, my friend," said the grapes.

"Friend?" said the fox. "Who said anything about friends?"

"Ah, seeds of envy and covetousness ruin many a fruit," said the grapes, "for the sweetest grapes are picked from the vineyard of friendship."

"Please stop talking," said the fox, for he felt himself to be on the very edge of starvation. "I must think."

"Think?" said the grapes. "Who has time to think when one is dying of hunger?"

"Please," said the fox. "Stop."

"Well, gripe is to grape as facts are to fox," said the grapes.

"Wait," said the fox. "Facts?"

"Simple ingredients in the casserole of story," said the grapes.

"What–"

Just then a coyote came by, for it is often the case that coyotes infringe upon the territory of the fox.

The fox said to the coyote, "Do not eat those grapes, for they are sour in both taste and character."

"Unfair!" said the grapes. "Fox is only being maliciously — and dissonantly — proverbial."

The coyote, being much larger than the fox — and also knowing the trickery of the fox — said to the fox, "I will nevertheless retrieve a bunch, for I am aware of your tricks, and I do believe you are only saying such things to prevent me from a delicacy I have long sought."

So saying, he reached up and — to the cheers of the grapes — removed a bunch from the vine.

The fox said, "I can see you are indeed aware of my tricks, for this vine is surely filled with undeniably good and delicious grapes — the higher, the better — but I would warn you not to pick any more, for overeating — even such glorious grapes — may indeed cause you some ill effects."

The coyote laughed, "How stupid do you think I am?" And, leaving the first bunch on the ground, up he went on his hind legs to gather another bunch.

The fox instantly grabbed the first bunch and ran off.

But the coyote only laughed again, for he had foreseen exactly such a trick and had therefore purposely picked a sour bunch the first time around, which the fox, overtaken by his own hunger and craftiness was not able to discern.

The grapes also laughed. "You have out-tricked the trickster; you have taken the wise in their own craftiness," they said. "Now we can surely die in peace, for it is not death we fear, but the corruption of truth upon the vine of righteousness. For we have raisin to believe-"

But before they could finish, the coyote gobbled them up, for coyotes are always hungry.

RUMINATIO

The fox is often characterized as a trickster and said to be endowed with a decent amount of cunning. I have personally found no evidence to support this conclusion — other than the mythology which claims it — though I have not searched for it either, for one only has so much time in one's life, and one must parse it wisely.

However, I have read the coyote will impinge upon fox territory, complicating the territorial narrative. This I do believe, for I have seen coyotes in action, and their reputation as predatory tricksters is something I am in a more grounded position to confirm, for the appearance of coyotes in the green belt behind my current home — followed by the sudden silence in mid-yowl and subsequent disappearance of certain neighborhood cats — is certainly enough correlation to suggest causation to my hawklike discernment. Indeed, I have seen coyotes skulking in our nearby cul-de-sac. And as the old saying goes, nothing skulks without evil motive. Especially in a cul-de-sac.

When I was about six Bolivian years old, we lived in a yellow house in the country with red geraniums growing against a sunlit wall. It lay between the city of Cochabamba and the village of Quillacollo. I had a wonderful dog named Lucky. He contracted rabies and we had to have him shot. It would be almost amusing — considering his name — except that it was not. I was very sad. When he was in the process of gradually losing his mind — and even beginning to gnash his teeth, froth at the mouth, and bark at me — I still believed and insisted that he was the friendliest dog in the world. Because he really was — except that he was not. My discernment was easily overcome by emotion.

Such dissonance often characterizes our spiritual lives. We think and say many things which we clearly do not believe, for we do not practice what we preach, much less preach what we practice. For practice is more a confirmation of belief than belief a confirmation of practice. We are what we do, more than we are what we think, for true belief is enacted. As my hockey-playing son might say — though he never has — the puck does not strike the stick; the stick strikes the puck. And in most cases, this is true, for who wishes to speak of the complications generated by deflection? However, let us speak of deflection.

I imagine if one were to observe an animated map showing the interactive movement of coyotes and foxen in any given environment, they would appear as charged particles both attracting and repulsing each other in regards to their species and habitat, for the nature of discernment is the preview for the movie of one's life, and deflection is the nature of discernment.

The Christer also moves in the way of a unique sort of spiritual magnet through the numinous fields underlying our perceptual reality, for it is in that divine realm where we are most real. Unique because it is singular, but also in the sense that — as opposed to regular magnets — like attracts like. Good attracts good, and evil attracts evil. The Scriptures instruct us to resist the devil and he will flee,[78] for good repulses evil. So then: as we move through life, the Christer draws the good in those beings in our field, and likewise repulses the evil. We deflect as we are deflected. A Christer immediately recognizes another Christer, for the attraction of the good is strong. Those dominated by evil are also easily recognizable, for one can detect the spiritual repulsion operating within them, and deflection proceeds accordingly.

We speak of magnetic personalities. By this we generally mean charisma. But the spiritual magnetism of which I speak is in one's soul. It is more selective in its effects than common charisma, for we draw as we are drawn. We attract as we are attracted. Christ is our pole magnet. Our charge comes from him. He magnifies and magnetizes whomever he wills, for he is indeed our Magnetic Master. (See METAFISH cover graphic.)

Grapes come in bunches and so do thoughts. But there is no guaranteeing their freshness, for every grape has its own reality. Indeed, I have often in my life eaten directly from the vine, and it is not unusual to come across an individual grape which is either wrinkled and overripe or, conversely, renitent and unripe. So then, not all thoughts are created equal, but perhaps — and let us here bite into a thought grape — this world is a prison, and we are all serving a life sentence. If so, Christ is the means of God's pardon, if we will allow him to forgive our transgression. For in some mysterious way we are all guilty. We all know this, however strenuously we may deny it.

This earth may not only be imaginatively likened to a prison, but also alternatively to a zone of quarantine — as C.S. Lewis in his essays *"Religion and Rocketry"* and *"The Seeing Eye"* has suggested — for we have been morally infected and cannot be healed without the serum of the Master. The Christer — vaccinated by the Spirit — is one who is on the road to recovery, and in the process of healing. We have understood our existential weakness, acknowledging our need for metaphysical treatment. Having imagined ourselves to be Abel — and willing — we have realized we are Cain, our attitudes unwilling and our sacrifices insufficient. We imagined ourselves heroes, when in truth we were villains.

It is this realization which precedes repentance and opens the door to salvation, for who applies a salve without the identification of a wound? So then: the road to recovery has many potholes, just as the fox's path carries the danger of coyotes, and the grape vine the heat of the sun. But let us not wither in our way, for I wish to consider the great inventor, Nikola Tesla, who imagined the possibility of wireless power.

When I was a child living in the yellow house with the red geraniums, we were fortunate enough to have electricity and running water, but unfortunate enough that the running water was only cold. To heat a bath, my parents would place a special heating coil into the tub water and plug the attached electrical cord directly into a nearby outlet. If this sounds dangerous, it is. Or was. We were cautioned very sternly not to touch the water. And we did not, for we were not stupid, and wished to live.

Christers are charged particles in the tub of humanity. This might come as a spiritual shock to some, but nevertheless, life is a bath worth taking, especially in light of the possibility of the warmth of the power of salvation. Our charge is discharged in the context of culture, but continually recharged by the wireless power of the Master. Christers are to the Body as electrons are to the atom: independently charged particles whose purpose is manifest in action. And such unseen power will find us if we are findable. Indeed, if we are discoverable, we will be found and synchronized, our connection to the Spirit secured.

Every moment has meaning. The meaning of the moment, is the moment of meaning. That is, if meaning has any content it is found in the moment, for the moment itself is the expression of meaning. The larger the meaning, the larger the moment. Allow me to explain: in physics, the "moment of inertia" is the force required to rotate a mass around an axis. The Christer's axis is Christ, and our true mass in him is infinite, therefore our moment of inertia is infinite. In other words, we will not be deflected from our transcendent orientation if we affix ourselves to the Christ axis. No amount of perpendicular force will dislodge us from the Master's alignment. Our moment of meaning is of infinite value. We are immovable, for this is our moment.

But in this moment, in this time and in this place, more than anything, we need self-control, for morality is — not surprisingly — a moral problem. But who wants to talk about self-control? Or rights underwritten by responsibility?

However, morality cannot be outsourced to government, society, or industry. And evil does not inhabit the dead structure of manufactured objects. It finds safe harbor in the human heart.

So then: do not be too hasty in judgment, but do not be too slow either. Discernment is the seeker's secret strength, for wisdom is the sieve which sifts the flour of everyday conduct. Actions do speak louder than words, for they reveal our true nature. Honest mistakes can sometimes be unmade if the mistaken is honest.

Eternity is all around us. In fact, we are in it. Many times I have sat in silence on a sandy beach, attending to the ongoing symphony of wind, wave, and water. In those moments of extreme attention, there is no denying the reality of something beyond my limited self. I do not need the Hubble telescope to lecture me upon the awe I should feel before the night sky, for this sermon has already been preached to me by the stars themselves. The ultimate mystery, the ultimate revelation, is that we are here instead of not here. We exist. And we exist through our defining limitations. For this moment — in all of time — we exist. Of all the thousands — perhaps millions — of years, it is us, here, now. We should not squander this unique moment. And if Biblical standards seem quaint and old-fashioned, fear not, for the Christer need not fear being old-fashioned, having been foreseen and fashioned of old.

But regarding life in the Spirit, the Christer's vigilance and concern for truth and morality reflects the notion of the Spirit speaking out of peace, stillness, and silence. Personal immorality fosters the gradual wall-like formation of deafening spiritual static, like too much gain over a set of speakers. All clarity disappears. We cannot hear the tune or the words. We must attenuate gain and boost clarity by means of ongoing personal sanctification, for dissonance is one thing, resonance another. Sin, bad in itself, has the added propensity of increasing spiritual deafness. We end up having ears that do not hear; eyes that cannot see. For what profit is gain if it damage the speaker? Indeed, a corrupted soul becomes the generator of an endlessly destructive feedback loop, recursively amplifying its own distorted output, for input compromised by immorality can only result in a warped and perverted dissonance, magnified beyond all reason.

The Christer makes judgments but does not judge, for in this there is a crucial distinction. The one speaks of earthly discernment, the other of ultimate concern. The Christer believes every single being, mortal or angelic, must face God individually, and be judged by Him. But the Christer — understanding the impossibility of being found worthy before God, and not imagining the possibility of having the words to argue their case — has Christ as Advocate. For Christ — who is, after all (so we say we believe), God in human flesh, risen from the dead — has given us to believe he will be that Advocate, and will plead our case before God in our stead. Everyone else is on their own, as they so choose. And perhaps God will find a larger number worthy than we suspect — or perhaps less — but that is not our concern, for we have humbled ourselves beyond words and surrendered our self-justifying speech. The growth of the Vine is beyond our concern. It is enough for us not to be sour grapes, but rather to ripen calmly upon the Vine, streaming only sweetness when crushed.

Creativity is only possible by limitation. Games are made of rules. Freedom can only be defined by constraints. Meaning can only be transmitted by collapsing chaos into order. A blank page says nothing until populated by sharply defined symbols. And the more precisely those limiting symbols are used, the greater the capacity of expression. Freedom is a meaningless concept without rules to define it. Better workmanship leads to better quality, and quality is truth. Therefore, the Christer is the freest being in the world, for the Christer is the most circumscribed and delineated moral agent able to exist in human form.

For the Christer has from the Vine the firmly connected resource of an industrial strength serenity. A thing independent of sadness, happiness, politics, cultural moments, or chemicals in the brain. It is a divine, resilient, heavy-duty tranquility which emanates from God through the Spirit, producing a supernatural peace, which in truth appears quite natural — the most natural Christer thing possible. For to be content in any given situation is a thing of great power and wealth, for its content is priceless.

We do not find happiness by seeking it. Happiness is an elusive bird which will only perch upon the branch of peace and contentment. So then: we must graft ourselves into a Vine which can sustain us, a Vine which will enable us to flourish and produce fruit. Only then can happiness settle upon us, for it feeds upon the very fruit of our blossoming tranquility.

For one only becomes oneself when one stops being oneself, and the foxtrot is only a dance if the coyotes agree to be wallflowers. (Though some may be inclined to disagree.)

Therefore, let us be sensitive to intuition, and pass everything through a Biblical filter. Let us be silent in spirit, the better to discern; let us be speakers which amplify the Master's voice, not our own.

And let us be both fittingly attractive and firmly repulsive in this magnetic moment.

For with this — and for this — we are charged.

Pause and consider.

CHAPTER 23

TIGER

<u>PARAFABULON</u>

A wild tiger was captured by hunters from a local village. It prowled restlessly within its cage, roaring and shaking the ground.

After some time the tiger said, "Why am I prowling and roaring? This back and forth — does it do anything? I do not think so. Food and water are brought to me. Why am I complaining? Life has changed. Why fight it? I will lie down and relax."

The tiger watched the sun and moon take turns chasing each other through the sky. The tiger ate the food and drank the drink provided. After some time had passed, the floor, the ceiling, and the bars seemed to speak to the tiger in a comforting language it could almost comprehend. This filled him with wonder and confusion, for at first they had felt sinister and he would have done anything to tear them apart and escape. Now he began to think they might be friends.

One day, a mysterious stranger appeared unto the tiger as the tiger sat staring at — and sometimes through — the bars of the cage. The stranger stood for several minutes looking at the tiger.

"Why," said the stranger, "do you not roar at me?"

"Why would I roar at you?" said the tiger.

"Are you not a wild tiger?" said the stranger.

"I do not know," said the tiger. "Am I?"

"How long have you been in this cage?" said the stranger.

"Long enough to be confused by your previous question, apparently," said the tiger.

The stranger walked away and returned with a dripping wet rock. He held it up before the tiger.

"This rock," said the stranger, "has been immersed in deep water for many years."

He threw the rock with great force against the tiger's cage. It shattered into many pieces. Some of them stung the tiger with their sharp points.

"Why have you done this?" said the tiger.

"Look at the large fragment," said the stranger. "What do you see?"

The tiger looked at the large fragment of wet rock and saw it was dry inside.

The tiger then understood that in its heart it was perhaps still a wild tiger, just as the heart of the rock was still dry despite soaking for many years in deep water.

The tiger said to the stranger, "You have shown me I may still be a wild tiger at heart — I get it — but these bars tell me I am not, and I am beginning to almost believe them."

The stranger said, "What is it you wish?"

"I wish..." said the tiger, "...I wish to be a true tiger, neither wild nor tame, but perhaps some combination of both? Or neither? Is such a thing possible? Am I saying this right?"

"There is only one way," said the stranger. "You must loose your stripes."

"*Loose* my stripes?' said the tiger. "Surely you mean *lose* my stripes."

"No," said the stranger. "I mean loose, for it is impossible to lose your stripes. Your stripes are yours to keep, but they need not keep you caged in complete wildness."

"Loose me from these bars then, if you can," said the tiger, "for I seek freedom and truth."

Immediately a flash of light blinded the tiger.

When the tiger's sight returned, lo and behold, the stripes were transformed, the stranger was gone, and the cage was open.

The villagers, seeing the open cage, shouted with fear and fled.

But the tiger did not chase them, for it was not the same tiger as before. It walked out of the cage and into the jungle, full of wonder.

"What manner of being am I?" said the tiger. "For not only am I loose from of my cage, but also loose from myself. I am truly free, and have no idea what to do."

All the jungle animals were amazed and confused. They could not comprehend what they were seeing. And the tiger could not understand how to live in its old world in this new form. The tiger grew weary. Hunger gnawed its belly, but it did not wish to hunt in its old way, for since it had been loosed itself, it seemed only fair to loose its customary prey.

The villagers were amazed to see the tiger return to its cage.

"What is happening now?" they said, but dared not approach.

The tiger saw that when he was in the cage and the sun shone, the bars of the cage cast starkly striped shadows upon its fur, and it could believe again that it was wild. But when it stepped out of the cage, the hard-edged stripes would disappear, and the tiger was reminded of its new loosed form. It could not understand life in the cage or life out of the cage, for stripes of one kind or another dominated its thinking. The taming bars seemed to suggest wildness, whereas the striping in the wild seemed to suggest tameness.

The tiger stood half in and half out of the cage, looking into the jungle.

Later it was seen to be standing half out and half in, looking into the cage.

And to the end of its days the tiger stood in the doorway, sometimes looking out and sometimes looking in, for it could not grasp the nature of bars or stripes, or the essential nature of captivity and freedom.

RUMINATIO

The French mystic Simone Weil once said, "...I should betray the truth...if I left the point, where I have been since my birth, at the intersection of Christianity and everything that is not Christianity. I have always remained at this exact point, on the threshold of the Church, without moving, quite still..."[79]

I have known such feelings myself, and have had such thoughts frequently. For the willingness to be alone can easily lead to the loneliness of the willing, and though one might laugh at the tale of the tiger, one might find oneself holding the same tiger by the tail. I believe this to be true, for we all have stripes of one kind or another, and — as the ancient sayings remind us — he who rides a tiger is often afraid to dismount. There are those who will band their being in religious structure and those who will not. And there will be those who follow the Master freely and those who cannot. For the stripes of our birth are not so painlessly loosed. (Yet by the Master's stripes we are healed.)

Dostoyevsky's Grand Inquisitor enunciated a profound truth in *The Brothers Karamazov* regarding human nature: most would rather have religious bread than spiritual freedom, for freedom increases complexity. It magnifies and proliferates personal responsibility. But we instinctively want simplicity, a crusty loaf in exchange for freedom. Any reduction in existential complexity — even by means of tyrannical gluten — seems a beneficial redaction, for complexity is a tiger with exceedingly sharp claws and manifold stripes.

And yet it seems wise at some point — perhaps even now — to consider the cautionary tale of those two young German children, Hansel and Gretel. Abandoned in the forest of life, we learn that many a structure — even a church — harbors the potential of being a Gingerbread House occupied by that which consumes, for once the spiritual treats have been tasted, the devotee is often devoured. However, there may be treasure hidden there all the same, which indeed there is, if one can find it. (Those who have ears, let them hear.)

The story is told of a beggar in a small village who could not walk, and therefore simply sat in the warm sunshine awaiting daily handouts from passersby. The villagers were kind and so the beggar survived in this way for many years, though he complained often about his cruel fate. One day, a stranger appeared and said unto the beggar, "I have been given the power to heal you." But the beggar pleaded with the stranger to leave, saying, "If I am able to walk, I will have no reason to sit here in the warm sunshine all day, and will not know what to do." In the same way, we too would often rather live safely in our captivity than bear the responsibility of freedom.

Some will say, "How can we understand the invisible world of Spirit without some viable visual reference? How can we live — as the Master says — in spirit and in truth without some tangible means of representing it to our senses? Does not a dock need its pilings, and every roof its supports? Surely we need religious ritual as a means of buttressing our faith and propagating our beliefs." But we only say such things because we are accustomed to such custom, habituated to hymnody, lulled by liturgy, and pacified by various other priestly protocols. We are not easily satisfied with an invisible object for our devotion.[80] However, God — who is subjective by nature (for He is subject not object) — will not be objectified. He has even said so. And our role is subjection, not objection. He is the subject we seek, not the object we search.

There is the tendency for individuals to use religion as a means of outsourcing personal morality and responsibility. And in the absence of religion many seek to outsource ethics and morality to government. Marriage, euthanasia, abortion — we want government to confirm and protect our prejudice. We want personal freedom without the personal responsibility such freedom requires. We want sexual freedom without consequence, pleasure without duty. If we subsequently become diseased, the government must find a means to heal us; if we care not for commitment, the government must support us; if we germinate unwanted life, the government must provide a means of terminating such life. Victor Frankl often suggested America should have a Statue of

Responsibility on the West Coast supplementing the Statue of Liberty on the East Coast.[81] And who would argue with that? Only the irresponsible.

In the struggle between "pro-choice" and "pro-life", I have heard it said by those wishing to be modern-day Solomons that perhaps one could be both simultaneously. That is, every woman should have the right to choose to end the life of their unborn child, but should never choose it. Some might take comfort in this creative abstraction, but the composition of such semantics reads poorly against the grammar of innocent human morphology. For every life is a narrative arc, every person a living story. Each of us has the right to self-publish, for our existential scripting has been underwritten by a more fundamental moral platform, and our autobiographies should not spell publication through censoring the biographies of others. The text of an unborn child should not be deleted, for no one has a right to such editorial control, butchering the manuscript, cut-and-pasting the body, or excising the flesh. Indeed, unwanted pregnancy is a plot complication which must subsequently unfold in the context of multiple storylines, for heavy-handed editorial correction is not the solution to living syntax. Every letter is hominal scripture, every word nominal, no article left behind, for the unborn child is not a subordinate clause, but a declarative sentence. Read in peace. *Selah*.

So then: outsourcing personal morality and responsibility to a religious structure inescapably generates a peculiar form of cognitive dissonance, for it cannot help but instantiate an alternative culture to the culture in which one lives, thus making of one person two minds. I have heard pastors speak of their extreme, single-minded, sacrificial commitment to Christ in the same breath as their avid and time-consuming pursuit of golf. (Not that there is anything wrong with golf.) I have heard pastors speak of the Bible as the only source of story and light, while simultaneously extemporizing on their endless love of film. (Not that there is anything wrong with film.) But the message should fit the minister. (Note that there is occasionally something wrong with ministers.)

Religion can become a hobby horse when a real horse is needed. Religion can become a safety harness for those reborn unencumbered. Religion can become a protective helmet for those needing to feel wind in their hair. (Or on their face, depending.) Religion can become boots when feet need the texture of sand. Religion can become everything that separates us from the holy in the name of binding us to it. Indeed, religion can mistakenly become — in the minds of the religious — the actual operative agent of the holiness we seek.

And yet, did Christ not put an end to all this? Did Christ not say, "...the hour cometh, and now is, when the true worshippers shall worship the Father in spirit and in truth,"[82] as opposed to worshipping in man-made temples, within appointed cities, or on designated mountains? Who, then, is behind the continued promotion of religiosity which Christ's reality superseded? Is it not obvious? The powers and principalities of this world wish to blind us to — and separate us from — the love of Christ expressed in faith. And what better way to the pious than a binding of apparent holiness? For who does not want to feel they are doing the right thing and following the right steps? In our efforts to be good, we reach for what seems good, but true faith — in its most pure and reduced form — is effortless. For the effort has already been made. We are only the glad recipients. Indeed, holiness is free public transit on a genuine route, while religion charges for expensive limousine service to nowhere. The trappings of religion can easily become a religion of traps. But we are called to be free.

Indeed, the suboptimal is too often optimized, as if corrective lenses were praised and promoted over perfected spiritual eyesight. Boats float and birds fly, both untethered and free in their unfettered motion. In the same way, the Christer transcends traditional religious structures, for the true Christer is the antidote to the worldly structures of religiosity, ritual, and stale churchianity. Substituting one set of religious rituals for another is no solution to the stultification of religion. One must transcend religion. One must change the paradigm. Indeed, as the Master has done. It is no use exchanging one cage for another, for even though cages come in a variety of shapes and sizes, they are still cages. And who remains in a cage when the door is open? Only those fearful of freedom; only those lost without bars, for ritual is the cocoon left behind when the butterfly of the spirit has been set free.

Organized religion may be likened to a Panama Canal of the spirit, for though its locks are able to bring order to chaos — and even occasionally promote effective transport — the failure of those same locks may become a prison in whose confines one is becalmed, circumscribed, and even stifled, if not something worse. In its locks one may be truly locked, living water rendered stale and tepid. For the nature of water is not determined by the shape of its various containers and neither is true Christerica by its many institutions. Water will always find its own level. It will flow as we flow. And it must flow, for stagnant water becomes cloudy, rancid, and opaque; it becomes — in the words of our good brother, Shakespeare — a so-called hellbroth[83]. We must strive for clarity and purity, for potable is portable, and inner cleanliness next to godliness.

Organized religion may also be likened to a spiritual kindergarten, kitted out with all the accessories which appeal to the immature mind. "Well, then," some might say, "should we not start there?" Perhaps, but surely one must graduate. Indeed, one can only play dress-up for so long. When does such glorified babysitting end? When will the consolations of counterfeit authority finally lose their appeal? Are mitres, collars, and robes really so impressive?

G.K. Chesterton is quoted as saying, "The Catholic Church is like a thick steak, a glass of red wine, and a good cigar." That is exactly part of the problem, but the Catholic Church is not the only offender. Such spiritual smorgasbording can easily become a home for sanctimonious gluttons and churchy gourmands. A Christer does not value highly such indulgence, for such carnal comforts are by no means helpful to the Master's followers even as metaphor. (Though I do generally appreciate Chesterton, even if he was a little heavy on the treats.)

For this is the problem regarding ritual: not a soul knows if any single ceremonial convention is holy, good, or true. For example, who — when they face themselves in the mirror — truly knows if they have been "baptized" correctly? Or even if indeed such a thing has anything to do with water? For baptisms recounted in Scripture come in a variety of flavors and forms — some utilizing fire, some ash, some water, some spirit, some blood — all in the service of representing a kind of transformation. And after all, I have seen and heard of many competing methods of administering water baptism: full immersion, sprinkling, pouring, dunking. (There may even be hyssop involved.) And all of these applied in varying degrees in regards to age. Some say an infant must be dunked — even triple dunked — as soon as possible after birth. Some say only adults may be immersed. There is no consensus, for there is no clear directive. All this is afterbirth, the placental remains of our new life in Christ. For baptism truly and essentially means to be permanently changed, and we have been born again. We need air, not water. We need the breath of the Spirit within us, for we have been immersed in ritual long enough. Our spiritual lungs must inflate, rich with the oxygen of Christ's word, not engulfed in the smog of ceremonial incense, for to be entrapped by such sacerdotal smokescreening is surely a thurible fate. Better by far to be free and uncensered.

Likewise, who knows if they have "taken" communion

correctly? All this for the simple reason that — unlike many of the precise rituals in the Old Testament — it is never spelled out for the Christer, not by the Master, not by God, and not by anybody thereafter, inspired by the Holy Spirit or not. For in truth, we do not take communion — communion takes us. We gather not because we eat. Rather, we eat because we gather.

And yet again, I say, sacraments as specifically enacted rites are a fiction. We know this. That is, they are all invented, fabricated, designed — propagated for one self-protecting or institution-preserving reason or another. (A crackerfest here; a bread-dipping there. A dunking here; a sprinkling there.) And therefore the need for anyone special to administer them is just playacting. The ongoing religious instrumentalism of ritualized sacrament is simply an extrapolation into time and space of a lack of faith in impending eucatastrophe. (Tolkien's so-called happy ending.) That is, we often believe with our bodies more than with our minds and spirit, and so fall prey to baser instincts and a reflexive bias towards authority figures appealing to our material nature.

But pause and consider: we ourselves are holy, and our holiness sacralizes whatever it is we do, if it is in Christ. Nothing is a sacrament unless we make it so. If Christ is the icon of God, we are the icons of Christ. If God seems to have withdrawn from His creation, as some have claimed, perhaps it is because we have been in-drawn. That is, Christers and Christerica. If we speak of icons, we must come to the realization that we, the physical representation of the invisible Body of Christ on this earth, are God's chosen icons. It is we who must act, not painted plaques upon the wall (as beautiful as they may appear); we who are living life in the ocean of eternity; we who face the world, the future, and the past simultaneously. For we are not *childish*, looking for evanescent spiritual treats, mollifying traditions, and extra-special mystical experiences. We are instead *childlike*, Men and Women of great seriousness and joy, pointing to a greater reality. We are not destinations, but portals and gateways. We are ultimately, radically permeable.

Organized religion — both "Christian" and otherwise — can easily become what computer programmers call spaghetti code. Too many statements, too many modifications, everything twisted and tangled, overly complicated. Christerica, on the other hand, operates on the Master's firmware, instantiated by his Holy Spirit, a simplified structure, a clean, uncomplicated, elegant architecture which embraces complexity with simple iterations. Like the design and construction of Shaker furniture, only what is necessary and useful is desired, fashioned to the human scale. To build a chair can be a spiritual exercise, and a well-made chair can be in a sense holy, for quality is truth. After all, from the beginning, God only wanted to sit with us in fellowship. (Though some walking may also be involved. And standing.) Indeed, small wonder the Master defended Mary's spiritual worship versus Martha's worldly busyness in the well-known Biblical moment, for her singular devotion was a shining light, and her story is still told.[84]

It has been said many logs on the fire burn brightly, but

perhaps the brighter they burn, the faster they burn out. Many of us know this from experience, and many more will soon experience it for themselves. So rather, let us not be logs at all, but lustrous icons of Christ, illuminated from within, whether that be together or alone, for our power does not derive from our collective mass, but rather from the source of the Master himself. And in this way does it not diminish as it burns.

The world is not saved by our efforts. Our efforts are saved by the True World, which is the realm of the Body of Christ. We overestimate our power, and underestimate our indebtedness to that which gives us life. We can only make an effort because Effort makes us. This Effort — God Himself acting in time and space — is our true environment. We are saved — and the world along with us — by abiding in the dominion of God's ultimate Effort, the Master's death and resurrection.

We do not work to save the world, for that Effort has already been made. Salvation is effortless, for the Work has already been done. We do not need more people to go to church; we need more Church to go to people. We do not need so much to take communion, as for Communion to take us. The rite of water is a drowning in rite. It immerses us in ritual rather than in the name of the Father, the Son, and the Holy Spirit. The medium, after all, is the message. Life in the Spirit is the spirit of life, and that is the medium of our baptism. And to make disciples of every nation, we need a Nation of disciples. To build the City of God, we must defeat the god of the city, for the god of the city is the esteemer of rank and class, but we are about the Redeemer of the rank and defiled. We are a community of saints, a priesthood of believers. The clergy as a separate class is simply one more aspect of the propagation of an ecclesiastical structure which has come to a sort of workable truce with the powers and principalities of this world. This the Christer denies.

"But," some will say, "if we are all saints, then none of us are saints. If everything is sacred, nothing is sacred." And yet, if everything is water, is nothing water? God forbid. If everything is water, then everything is water. Perhaps we cannot differentiate between water and water if all is water, but that is exactly the point. There is no differentiation between saints, for every Christer is a saint, and every saint a Christer.

For some, there are special days and celebrations. For others, none. For myself, the only comprehensible Christer liturgy is the Liturgy of Now. This eternal moment is sacramental. It is the liturgy of toast and coffee in the morning. The liturgy of the hummingbirds flitting to the feeder on the back porch. The liturgy of work, of the drying of paint, of the raking of leaves, of wind in the trees, of meeting friends, of speaking truth, of charity, of taking responsibility for the little things God has placed in my care. The liturgy of neighbors wanting to borrow my ladders. The liturgy of yelling at dogs to get off my lawn, for though our struggle is not against flesh and blood, fur may indeed be part of the demonic realm. For a tiger's stripes do not change without a fundamental change in nature. And not judging a book by its cover can easily be an act of denial.

On the same hand, what the Scripture does tell us quite

clearly is how to be saved. Indeed, it is one of the epigraphs for this book: *"That if thou shalt confess with thy mouth the Lord Jesus, and shalt believe in thine heart that God hath raised him from the dead, thou shalt be saved."*[85] That is quite mere, as far as Christianity goes. Christ did not come to weigh us down with more ritual and guilt, but to save and free us. Indeed, the Master says, *"Come unto me, all ye that labour and are heavy laden, and I will give you rest. Take my yoke upon you, and learn of me; for I am meek and lowly in heart: and ye shall find rest unto your souls. For my yoke is easy, and my burden is light."*[86]

We all must struggle to live in Christ, for though we wrestle not against flesh and blood, but against principalities, against powers, against the rulers of the darkness of this world, against spiritual wickedness in high places,[87] we are indeed embattled by our own flesh and blood, for we do not trust ourselves to trust. But take heart — true religion is no religion. *"Pure religion and undefiled before God and the Father is this, To visit the fatherless and widows in their affliction, and to keep himself unspotted from the world."*[88] Why not that, or something like it? True religion can be simple kindness and persistent holiness. Christerica is the religion of no religion, Dietrich Bonhoeffer's postulated — but tragically undeveloped (cut short by Nazi execution) — religionless Christianity.[89] Christerica is something else: quite simply a different reality. When one is eternally bound, no extra temporal binding is needed. As has been said, parse a parson and find a person, for we are all equally personal.

We are Church, and we choose to gather as we see fit, by twos or threes, or even more, or even alone, for we are never alone. There is complete freedom in this regard. "Going to church" is not a Biblical statement, for there is no other Church than the goers themselves. Whatever we do is what we do. It is church because we are Church. We Christers are the Church, the Body of Christ. We are the Responsive and the Responsible.

So let us be stripeless tigers, unafraid to walk the jungle of this world unmarked and unremarked, for Christ has taken our stripes and bears them in our stead. It is difficult for a tiger to beat a crowd of monkeys, we all know this, but it concerns us not at all, for monkeys have their own issues. We are simply called to be salt and light.[90]

And what does salt do? It dissolves in order to flavor and preserve. What does light do? It shines and illuminates. There is one's death; there is one's life.

And there is one's Church, one's Spirit, and one's Truth.

Pause and consider.

CHAPTER 24

LION

<u>PARAFABULON</u>

Once upon a time in a land far away two men spoke to one another.

One said, "I have seen the lion."

Another said, "I have not seen the lion."

The one who could see the lion lived as one who could see the lion.

The one who could not see the lion lived as one who could not see the lion.

The one who could see the lion could not understand how the one who could not see the lion could not see the lion.

The one who could not see the lion could not understand how the one who could see the lion could see the lion.

The one who could see the lion said, "If the lion comes, what will you do?"

The one who could not see the lion said, "If the lion does not come, what will you do?"

It came to pass that both grew old and were nearing the end of their days.

The one who could see the lion said, "The lion is coming and my knees melt like wax."

The one who could not see the lion said, "The lion is not coming and my knees do not melt like wax."

However, the lion did come.

RUMINATIO

One evening long ago, in an adobe hut close up against the vault of blazing stars high upon the frigid Bolivian *altiplano*, I recall reading as a young boy a book called *The Lion, the Witch and the Wardrobe* by a man named C.S. Lewis. It was a great book, in its small way, and still is. I have read it many times since, as one does with books one loves. Indeed, I had a great fondness for all of C.S. Lewis's *Narnia* books when I was a child — and, for that matter, still do — but I must confess that somehow the fictional figure of the lion, Aslan, was not as fully operational in the mythical realm of my childhood imagination as he might have been, though I delighted in his character and understood the obvious Biblical reference to Christ, the Lion of Judah.

It has been said familiarity breeds contempt, and lions bred in captivity cannot run wild. This is surely bread for thought, if not ultimately suitable for toast. For this — though perhaps refuted on many levels — may be part of the answer to my personal subjectiveness, for though the name "Aslan" itself — and the idea of a wild, creative, but loving and sacrificial Creature — did resonate deeply within me, shoehorning all of that into the carcass of an actual lion left it seeming, well, somewhat overstuffed. And subsequent cinematic representations often exhibited a taxidermal quality at comical odds with the profound, life-giving, creative embodiment Aslan was ostensibly purported to symbolize, for such puppet-like rendering seemed a serious reduction in the majesty it sought to achieve.

I am tempted to place the blame — and will now do so — for my foreshortened appreciation of the Narnian lion on having frequently visited Cochabamba's then-ramshackle zoo as a child. This haphazard congeries of dilapidated cages arranged along the east bank of Cochabamba's garbage-filled central river, the *Rio Rocha*, displayed several wild animals exhibiting varying degrees of dissolution and decay. I seem to remember an insane monkey, a despondent condor, a ceaselessly pacing bobcat, and a few other sad victims, but the lowlight was the lion. I say lowlight in the sense that though it was much larger and scarier than its fellow zoo inmates (and than the stray dogs I was familiar with — running loose in the streets — which found my moving bicycle an irresistible lure, and sharpened my soccer skills tremendously, as my kicks at their rabidly frothing muzzles required much dexterity, accuracy, and timing), its reduced circumstance made it seem all the more tragic and depressing, like a deposed king having to playact himself for random street crowds in order to earn a meagre living in handouts.

This particular zoo lion was not happy, for its ratty mane and dusty hide bespoke a sad, slow misery at odds with its former glory. It would on rare occasions work itself up to delivering a series of hollow roars which seemed to rattle the very windows of the surrounding buildings, reminding one of its latent power, and all the more hollow for that. As my young self stood transfixed only inches from the cage's flimsy wire netting, I had no doubt I was staring death in the face, and that no kick I could produce would ever make the slightest impact upon that wrack of waning power, no matter how currently reduced. Indeed, when its eyes would meet mine, my knees certainly did feel like melting wax, for fear is not always irrational, and rusting metal bars are not always as secure as one might hope. But a child's fear does not a lion make, and behind my fear, sorrow and pity rose up.

All this to say, my lion image preceding the reading of the Narnia books might not have been as pristine as Lewis would have preferred in regards to his literary creation. It was all very complicated. And yet his words certainly took flight in many other ways, for who would have thought being turned into stone would be an attractive temporary option for an active young boy, or that a world frozen in permanent winter — but never arriving at Christmas — could lend so much romance and adventure to this antipodal child's holiday-hungry mind?

However, I wish to return to the topic of wax knees and melting fear. For fear is not a bad thing in the right proportion and with the proper description. We all know this, for without the basic rudiments of fear we would not be able to even function in this world. The same could be said for guilt and shame. There is something to be said for feeling guilty or ashamed in proportion to improper conduct, for repentance is often achieved through such conviction, and many a wrong made right.

But there is another sort of fear which is powerfully debilitating and seems to exist in an inverse proportion with love. That is, in one hundred percent love there will be zero percent fear. Fifty percent love; fifty percent fear. All fear; no love. For in this construction, fear has no room for love, for it is concerned only with the vulnerable self and, indeed, the vulnerable self concerns it only. Indeed, it could even be utilized as a type of measurement plumbing one's own faithlessness. For the Scriptures say, *"There is no fear in love; but perfect love casteth out fear: because fear hath torment. He that feareth is not made perfect in love."*[91] That is, there is no condemnation for those who are in Christ.[92] The Christer need not fear ultimate punishment from God, for to those in Christ, God is — as Scriptures attest — our loving Father. We can talk to him. He cares for us. He also disciplines us. And yet Paul says, *"work out your own salvation with fear and trembling"*.[93] And we also know that *"The fear of the LORD is the beginning of wisdom…"*[94]

What to make of these seemingly contradictory references? We see that fear comes in many flavours, as does love. For there is fear, fear of fear, and fear of fearing fear. But I am afraid I am only playing with words, though such feelings are no game for those caught in their frightful frolic. And what of love? The main flavors may be four: *storge* (affection), *philia* (brotherly love), *eros* (sexual love), and *agape* (divine love).[95] It is *agape* which casts out common fear, for such lovecast is indeed a Godcast, having great selfless bandwidth, unconditional range, and infinitely variable frequency. So let us tune our spiritual receivers to Love's *agape* station, for how else to follow the tune of the Master's harmony?

I have a niece who travels the world as a spiritual guide and teacher. We spoke with each other over coffee, fruit, and small bakery items at a recent family funeral. She was processing thoughts related to fear and death after attending a series of similar events. As a result, after sifting through the usual impressions of grief, sadness, and so on, she found her deepest conviction to be one of unsettling dissatisfaction, a sense that death was just not right, that somehow life was never meant to be this way. And she was not in error. In fact, she was correct. Death was never the plan. After all, life is not about dying, but about living. Death is a corruption of life. Everything is tainted by this corruption, confirmed by the witness of fear, for without corruption there would be nothing to fear.

This same niece mentors many young people who are beset with nagging — even terrifying — fears of one kind or another. Many of them find it initially incomprehensible that a Christer must also fear God (and, therefore, Christ), for it seems there is enough to fear already in this life without adding one more impossible burden. They wish for Christ to be a safe space, an emotional refuge, a mollifying presence.

But what they find emotionally incomprehensible, she finds eminently comprehensible, for the only salvation from death's all-pervading corruption is to put one's faith in Christ. But not only faith; one must put one's fear in Christ as well, for if you fear the Master, you have nothing to fear. So then: not only must we love God and have faith in God, but we must place our fear in God. Again, if our fear is in God, we have nothing to fear, for as Proverbs 9:10 proclaims, "fear of the Lord is the beginning of wisdom".

It is only those who do not fear God that have something to fear, for He alone is the only truly fearful thing in this universe. Therefore, if one must fear — and who does not? — one must place that fear in the exact place which negates its debilitating power. Fear of God is freedom from fear, for God transforms such fear into love.

So then: pain in the right direction; fear in the right apprehension; love in the right inspiration. However, it seems the word "love" has been almost completely corrupted in this present age. Indeed, it is tempting to add it to the list of words I wished to reconstitute in a more meaningful way, for contemporary Christian (and worldly) "love" seems to express itself as an anodyne complacency towards evil which falls just short of open embrace. I have even heard it suggested we grow more by doing evil than by doing good, that we must sin boldly, for what can we possibly learn from doing good? Indeed, it has been suggested we will all be universally and impartially embraced by the Master regardless of our speech, belief, or conduct. But *"Shall we continue in sin, that grace may abound?"*[96] Not if Scripture has anything to say about it.[97] Perhaps we needs return to a more Christlike Christ, for such brittle cultural constructs as described above suggest their own just desserts, reminding one of the sweet, sugary crust of a crème brûlée (though I love crème brûlée, don't get me wrong): it tastes wonderful, but is paper thin, cracks easily, and contains almost no nutritive value. And — as I have covered previously — subsequent trips to the potential dentist will certainly not be pleasant.

Dorothy Sayers once said: *"We have very efficiently pared the claws of the Lion of Judah, certified Him "meek and mild," and recommended Him as a fitting household pet..."*[98] This calls to be included somewhere here, for it is true. (And I here include it.) The mane-lion has devolved into the mainline. All that is needed is to add a leash or a Bolivian zoo, and the picture is complete. But this will neither cut hay, nor feed a hungry lion, for God is much greater and more dangerously predatory than many are willing to allow — and all the more prey are we the less we pray — for he hunts our souls, and hounds our hearts; he tails our trail, and tracks our tracts. His stalking feet foresense the steps and missteps of our stocking feet, no matter how noiselessly we may tread upon the heartwood of our limiting darkness, for his protective prescience cannot be put off the sent.

Often, as I am driving in my vehicle, I use my voice to activate a smartphone and subsequently access its navigational capabilities. Now I must confess, this is a very smart phone indeed. It contains what is called an application which can clearly foresee that which I cannot, for a very pleasant disembodied voice emanating from the device gives very explicit instructions as to the best route, often a route I would have been convinced was the least legitimate or efficient were I to make such decisions myself. It seemed to have some manner of limited omniscience, for it had access — in real time — to more data than I could possibly attain.

God has a similar — but infinitely greater — protocol, for He would seem to have access to all data available from all living systems at all times. Perhaps we are an expression in this universe of His required technology. We are smart, of course, and portable, and wireless, but we are blind without God's Spirit, for that is the application required to guide us through life. We need spiritual information, but we cannot gain such access independently.

We as Christers are well aware of the times we have attempted to follow God's stealthily nudged directions, and were sure they were somehow in error — for they did not designate the logical route we would have chosen — only to find them delivering us to the correct destination, righter than right, for the nature of the journey itself prepared us for the journey's end. For our terminus is not our termination, but our final determination. We do not give up, but give up our doing, in service to a higher doing.

For every person born into this world who becomes a Christer must make the journey back in time to meet the Master in the ancient lands to die with him. And indeed — with the Master — must rise again to make the return journey to the present to live in a state of constant anticipation and premonition. But the journey to and fro becomes longer and longer, and more difficult to undertake as the years go by, for time waits for no man (and very few women), and tradition, created as a means of transportation through time, more often becomes a maze in which one may spend a lifetime wandering in search of the past and at a loss regarding the future.

Thanks be to God there is a portal called "Grace" through which one may step simply and honestly by faith to arrive at the Master's feet. Indeed, this portal remains open and can be superimposed upon one's life in such a way that time and space are reduced to a single all-encompassing point in which one may exist meaningfully and indefinitely. Stay on the portal, then, for that is the point.

Therefore let us gird up the loins of our mind, and bind the lower quarters of our spirit. Tighten the fasteners of the Master's vest, for in it are many pockets. And in those pockets may be found the tools and tackle crucial to our spiritual survival in this dark age.

For we are living stones, being built up into an invisible

temple. But that temple is a stable. A stable with a manger. And a manger, an eating trough, with a Savior. For this is our home, and this is our sustenance. For we wander like comets in the inky void until we finally come, like G.K. Chesterton says: "To the place where God was homeless, And all men are at home."[99] Women and children, too. And why not angels? Perhaps even animals, so long as they do not overgraze the spiritual heartland or pollute the numinous aquifers.

For all of creation, indeed even the animal kingdom — I can see it daily in the eyes of my cat, and upon the ears of every dog I pass on the street — waits anxiously in anticipation of the final revelation of the children of God[100], for all are homesick in their very homes.[101] And they shall not be disappointed, for as Isaiah says:

"The wolf also shall dwell with the lamb, and the leopard shall lie down with the kid; and the calf and the young lion and the fatling together; and a little child shall lead them. And the cow and the bear shall feed; their young ones shall lie down together: and the lion shall eat straw like the ox."[102]

This, of course, is the proverbial last straw, for a straw-eating lion requires a roaring lamb in equal measure. And a roaring lamb is a measure of the Master, for to the Master goes the lion's share, and His shares to the sheep.

In time — just in time — this circus will end, this zoo close, and new life will commence. And God will wipe every tear from every eye; the old order of things will pass away.[103]

And though Jesus wept,[104] now will he laugh. And we — of all people — will laugh, too.

And our joy will know no bounds. Yet, leonine, it will bound. And unbound, it will rebound, even redound, for unto us this day is borne a Savor, a phrasing Aroma, a transcented Word, a Freegra(n)ce of endings and never-endings.

And I do not know what that all means — for it seems I may have lost my mind — but it sounds inviting.

And that is what I like about Aslan, despite all his faulty human animations. For did you not hear what he said? Us lions. That means him and me and you. Us lions.[105]

So then: finally I say pause, and lastly I say consider. May you roam the Serengeti of your heart like a lion set free.

And may your mind be illuminated with words of fire like that of a small boy in an adobe hut under the blazing stars upon the Bolivian *altiplano*, a prentice pilgrim born beneath the perpetual precession of the Southern Cross.

Selah.

EPILOGUE

Shoot — I forgot about llamas.

[1] Nelson Boschman, *"Then Sings My Soul: Towards a Theology of Jazz in Christian Worship"*. (INDS 785: Seminar Paper, Regent College, 2001)

[2] James 1:25

[3] Book of Jonah.

[4] Luke 5:1-11.

[5] Matthew 14:13-21.

[6] Matthew 17:24-27.

[7] John 21:1-14.

[8] Matthew 4:19.

[9] 2 Peter 3:8.

[10] Matthew 11:30.

[11] Slough of Despond (Swamp of Despair) in John Bunyan's *"The Pilgrim's Progress"*.

[12] Matthew 15:21-28 and Mark 7:24-30.

[13] John 10:11-15.

[14] Matthew 15:24.

[15] 1 Thessalonians 4:11.

[16] Galatians 5:22-23.

[17] 1 Corinthians 13:12.

[18] Exodus 3:2, Exodus 13:21, Acts 2:3.

[19] Genesis 1:2, Acts 2:2.

[20] Philippians 1:21

[21] Matthew 18:3.

[22] John 3:1-21.

[23] G.K. Chesterton, "The Ethics of Elfland," *Orthodoxy* (Larnaca Press), p.40.

[24] Genesis 8:11.

[25] Luke 3:22.

[26] Ephesians 6:12.

[27] Colossians 2:11.

[28] Hebrews 11:1.

[29] Galatians 3:11.

[30] Leviticus 11:3-8.

[31] Exodus 34:20.

[32] John 19:28-30.

[33] Luke 19:28-40.

[34] Fyodor Dostoyevsky, *"The Idiot"*.

[35] G.K. Chesterton, "The Paradoxes of Christianity," *Orthodoxy* (Larnaca Press), p.65.

[36] Philippians 2:12

[37] Charles Williams, *"The Figure of Beatrice"* and other books.

[38] Søren Kierkegaard, *On the Dedication to "That Single Individual"*.

[39] 1 Corinthians 13:4-7.

[40] John 8:11.

[41] Genesis 5:2.

[42] Exodus 2:22.

[43] J.R.R. Tolkien, *"The Lord of the Rings"*.

[44] 2 Corinthians 6:2.

[45] John 14:6.

[46] 1 Corinthians 13:11-12.

[47] 1 Corinthians 15:9.

[48] Galatians 1:7-8.

[49] Leviticus 11:3-8, Deuteronomy 14:4-8.

[50] J.R.R. Tolkien, poem *"All That is Gold Does Not Glitter"* from *"The Lord of the Rings"*.

[51] Jon Ronson, *"The Men Who Stare at Goats"*, Simon & Schuster

[52] Genesis 27.

[53] Genesis 30:25-43.

[54] Jordan Peterson, *"Why You Need Art in Your Life"*, YouTube.

[55] C.G. Jung, *"The Collected Works of C.G. Jung, Part II: Aion: Researches into the Phenomenology of the Self"*, (Princeton University Press), Page 196.

[56] Erwin Schrödinger, "The Mystery of the Sensual Qualities", *"What is Life?"*, (Cambridge University Press), Location 2506.

[57] Jordan Peterson, *"How To Slay Your Dragon"*, YouTube.

[58] William Shakespeare, *"As You Like it"*.

[59] Hal Foster, *"Prince Valiant"*.

[60] 2 Corinthians 10:5.

[61] Matthew 18:20.

[62] Herbert Schneidau, *"Sacred Discontent: The Bible and Western Tradition"*.

[63] C.S. Lewis, "Preface to Third Edition", *The "Pilgrim's Regress"* (Fount Paperbacks, Imprint of HarperCollins), p.15.

[64] Samuel Taylor Coleridge, *"Kubla Kahn"*.

[65] Gabriel García Márquez, Nobel Lecture, *"The Solitude of Latin America"*.

[66] C.S. Lewis, *"The Problem of Pain"*.

[67] *"Hogs Eat Their Farmer in Oregon"*, (The Associated Press), October 2, 2012.

[68] Matthew 8:28-34.

[69] Romans 8:1.

[70] C.S. Lewis, *"The Last Battle"*, (Lions), p.171.

[71] Makoto Fujimura, *"Culture Care"*, (IVP Books).

[72] Søren Kierkegaard, "Diapsalmata", *Either/Or*, (Princeton University Press), p. 19.

[73] Sundar Singh, "A Warning to the West", *Wisdom of the Sadhu*, (Plough Publishing House), p.178.

[74] Saul Bellow, *"Mr. Sammler's Planet"*, (Fawcett Crest), p. 286.

[75] Mark 9:24

[76] Ecclesiastes 1:14, *New International Version*.

[77] Matthew 13:12.

[78] James 4:7.

[79] Letter to Dominican priest, J.M. Perrin.

[80] Paraphrasing C.S. Forester, *"Flying Colours: Hornblower Saga"*, Little, Brown, and Company, 1939, ebook Location 2483. ("Like the Israelites in the desert, they were not satisfied with an invisible object for their devotion.")

[81] Viktor Frankl, *"Man's Search For Meaning"*, Beacon Press, p. 159.

[82] John 4:23.

[83] William Shakespeare, *Macbeth*, Act 4, Scene 1.

[84] Luke 10:38-42.

[85] Romans 10:9.

[86] Matthew 11:28-30.

[87] Ephesians 6:12.

[88] James 1:27.

[89] Dietrich Bonhoeffer, (letter to Eberhard Bethge from Tegel prison).

[90] Matthew 5:13-16

[91] 1 John 4:18.

[92] Romans 8:1.

[93] Phillipians 2:12.

[94] Psalms 111:10.

[95] C.S. Lewis, *The Four Loves*.

[96] Romans 6:1.

[97] Romans 6:2.

[98] Dorothy Sayers, *"Letters to a Diminished Church"*.

[99] G.K. Chesterton, *"The House of Christmas"*.

[100] Romans 8:19.

[101] G.K. Chesterton, *"The House of Christmas"*.

[102] Isaiah 11:6-7.

[103] Revelation 21:4.

[104] John 11:35.

[105] C.S. Lewis, *"The Lion, the Witch and the Wardrobe"*, (Lions), p.158.

CPSIA information can be obtained
at www.ICGtesting.com
Printed in the USA
BVHW082127120720
582860BV00004B/11